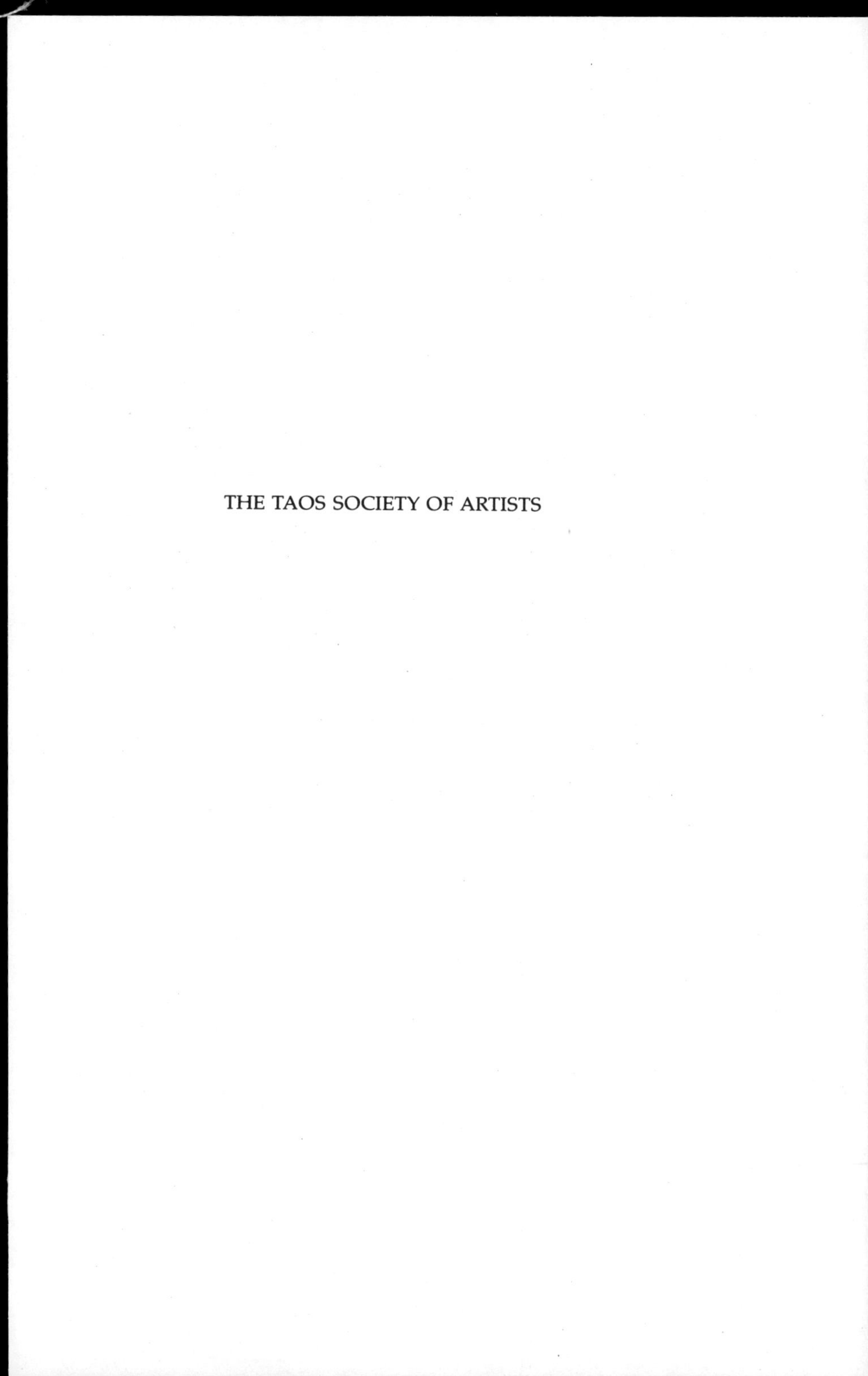

THE TAOS SOCIETY OF ARTISTS

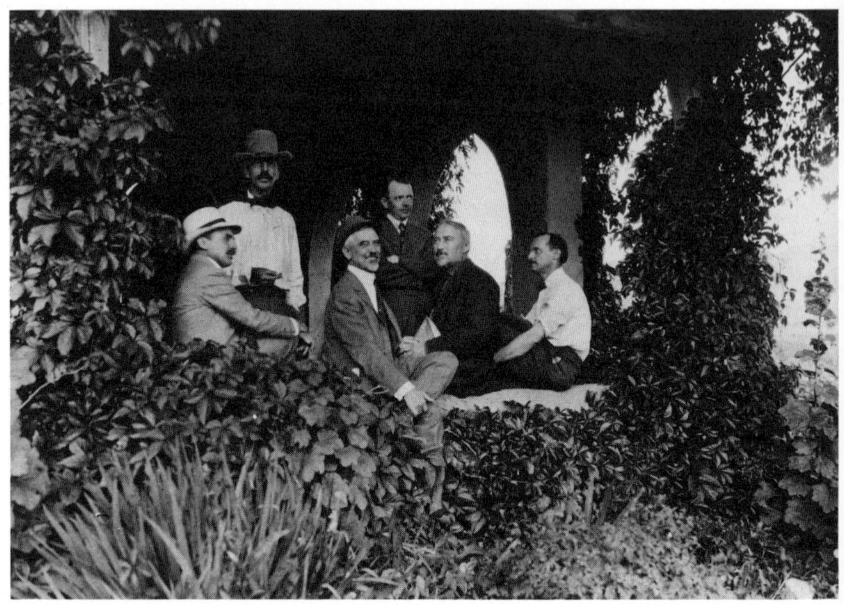

The six founding members of the Taos Society of Artists. From left to right: Bert G. Phillips, W. Herbert Dunton, Joseph Henry Sharp, Oscar E. Berninghaus, E. Irving Couse, and Ernest L. Blumenschein. Courtesy Museum of New Mexico (neg. no. 40399).

The TAOS SOCIETY of ARTISTS

Edited and Annotated by
Robert R. White

University of New Mexico Press / Albuquerque

Library of Congress Cataloging in Publication Data
Main entry under title
The Taos Society of Artists
Includes bibliographical references and index
1. Taos Society of Artists.
2. Art, Modern—
20th Century—New Mexico—Taos.
I. White, Robert R. (Robert Rankin), 1942– .
N6512.5.T34T36 1983 750′.6′078953 83-16939
ISBN 0-8263-1946-7

A first edition was published in 1983
by the University of New Mexico Press
in cooperation with
the Historical Society of New Mexico.

This book is dedicated
to the memory of
Mrs. E. Martin Hennings
(1893–1985)
and her daughter
Helen Hennings Winton
(1930–1990).

Contents

Illustrations

Illustrations

Publication of this book was made possible in part by a grant from Dr. and Mrs. William Stuart Wallace. The author would like to thank the Wallaces for their friendship and generosity.

Preface to the New Edition

In the fifteen years since the first edition of *The Taos Society of Artists* was published, art historians have done a great deal of research and writing on this subject. Scores of articles have appeared on the Taos Society of Artists and the individual members. Major books have been published on Couse, Higgins, Phillips, Berninghaus, Dunton, and Sharp.

Much new information has thus become available, and yet, much remains to be done. Previously unavailable documents have occasionally come to light through the years, and some of these have prompted reassessments of what actually happened in the early years of the Taos art colony. Conversely, some things have remained obscure, with no new information having surfaced to illuminate the course of events or the motivations of the participants. It is the purpose of this preface to briefly discuss some of the revisions in the scholarship on the art colony, to emphasize some of the events that particularly bear on the history of the Society, and to mention some of the questions that remain.

The Taos art colony was founded in 1898, but Blumenschein wrote that the stage was set several years earlier:

> I want to record the official beginning so will slip back a long time when I was an art student in Paris. There I met Henry Sharp. From him

I heard for the first time of the Indian village of Taos where he had sketched for a couple of weeks. It was located at the foot of a mountain in northern New Mexico. I remember being impressed, as I pigeon-holed that curious name in my memory with a hope that some day I might pass that way.[1]

Bert Phillips also first heard about Taos from Sharp in Paris, but Sharp may not have spoken with Phillips and Blumenschein about Taos at the same time. These three artists were in Paris to study at the Académie Julian, although they were not enrolled at exactly the same time. According to the records of the Académie, Phillips was enrolled in 1894, Blumenschein from 1894 to 1896, and Sharp in 1895 and 1896. As for an exact date for these conversations, the only firsthand evidence available is Blumenschein's statement that Sharp "told me of his visits to different tribes when I met him in Paris in '96, saying, that, as I was interested in Indians I should be sure to visit the Taos pueblo."[2]

Phillips and Blumenschein were in New York sharing a studio by the end of 1896. Much has been written about their arrival in Taos in September 1898, but that was not Blumenschein's first trip to the West. Late in 1897, Blumenschein received a commission from *McClure's Magazine* to illustrate a story relating to the Pima Reservation in southern Arizona. He left New York by train just before Christmas and arrived at Fort Wingate, in western New Mexico, on January 2, 1898. He stayed at Fort Wingate for two weeks. He attended a Navajo healing ceremony, which gave him an entirely different view of Native American culture than he had obtained from attending Buffalo Bill's Wild West show. He went to Arizona to complete his work on the Pima Reservation, but when he returned to New York in March, it was New Mexico rather than Arizona that had left an impression on his mind.[3]

Blumenschein went west again in early May 1898, this time

to Kansas, to meet William Allen White regarding the illustrations for one of White's stories for *McClure's Magazine*. Blumenschein was soon back in New York, and he and Phillips decided that the time had come for them to make a western trip together. They took the train to Denver, bought a wagon, horses, and equipment, and in the last week of May, they rode southward out of town. Phillips and Blumenschein camped and painted along the Front Range for most of the summer, but in August they headed for New Mexico. They had planned to go through Trinidad and follow the old Santa Fe Trail across Raton Pass, but south of Pueblo, Colorado, they met an old man who suggested that they cross the mountains into the San Luis Valley and then go southward to New Mexico. That was, in fact, what they did. The irony of this change in their route is that had they followed their original plan, they would have taken the Santa Fe Trail to Santa Fe and would have missed Taos altogether. It seems that the story about Sharp describing Taos to them took on greater importance in retrospect than it did at the time.

On the afternoon of September 3, 1898, when Phillips and Blumenschein were travelling through the mountains about 20 miles north of Taos, their wagon slid into a deep rut, and the left rear wheel collapsed. The flip of a three-dollar gold piece determined that Blumenschein would take the broken wheel to Taos for repair. He left at four o'clock that afternoon and returned two days later. On the following day, September 6, Phillips and Blumenschein arrived in Taos together. The delay caused by the broken wheel had given both of them time to look at the country and to decide that Taos was as far as they wanted to go.[4]

On October 19, 1898, the two artists attended a "progressive novelty party" in Taos at the home of Dr. and Mrs. Thomas P. Martin, given in honor of the doctor's sister, Rose, who was visiting from Shippensburg, Pennsylvania. About two weeks later,

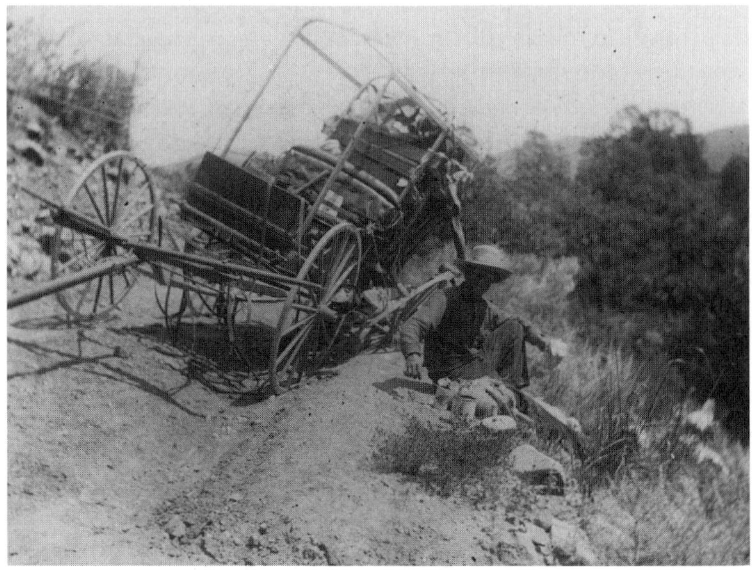

Ernest L. Blumenschein sitting beside the wagon with the broken wheel, September 3, 1898, about 20 miles north of Taos. Photo by Bert Phillips, courtesy Museum of New Mexico (neg. no. 40377).

a notice appeared in the Taos newspaper stating that Bert Phillips would teach art classes and that details could be obtained from his manager, Miss Rose Martin. It is apparent that a special relationship developed very quickly between Bert and Rose.[5]

Ernest Blumenschein left Taos on November 18, 1898, to return to New York and then to Paris. Phillips, however, kept finding reasons to delay his departure. In the spring of 1899, he proposed to Rose Martin, and they were married in Taos on Octo-

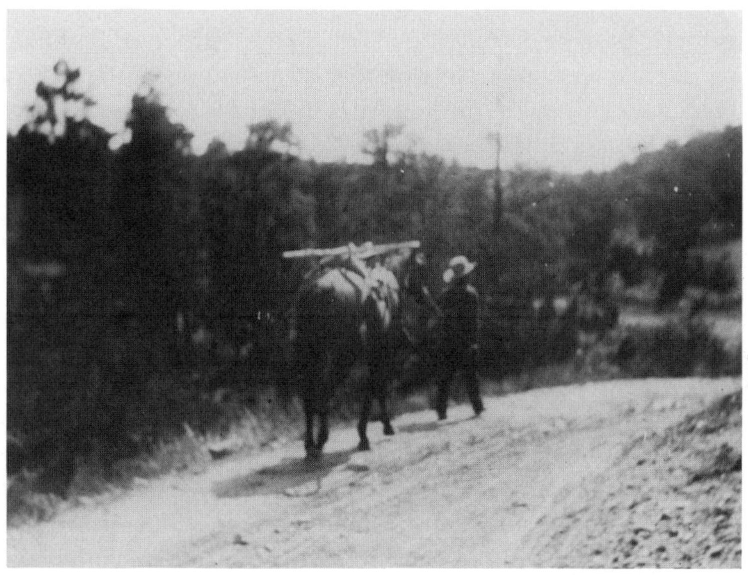

Ernest L. Blumenschein starting towards Taos with the broken wheel at 4:00 p.m. on September 3, 1898. Photo by Bert Phillips, courtesy Museum of New Mexico (neg. no. 40379).

ber 11, 1899. In later years, Phillips would attribute his decision to stay in Taos to the beautiful scenery, the clear mountain air, and the picturesque inhabitants, but the record strongly suggests that he remained in Taos during those first few months because he fell in love with Rose Martin.

By the time of his marriage, though, he had become fascinated with the Taos area and had resolved to settle there. He wanted other artists to join him. As early as September 1899, Phillips and Blumenschein were writing to each other about gathering people together in Taos "like the group of Barbizon painters & writers" (referring to the early nineteenth century French art colony). A message that Phillips is reported to have sent to Blumenschein best reveals his thoughts at this time: "For heavens sake tell people what we have found! Send some artists out here. There is a lifetime's work for twenty men. Anyhow, I'm lonesome."[6] Bert Phillips willingly took on the role of founder of the Taos art colony. For years he encouraged other artists to come to Taos, and he tirelessly promoted the idea of an art colony.

In January 1902, Bert Phillips received notice that he had been elected to the Society of Western Artists (SWA); his membership in this organization helped to shape his ideas about the future course of events in Taos. Formed in 1896, the SWA had chapters in various midwestern cities; Phillips became affiliated with the St. Louis chapter. Future Taos residents Oscar E. Berninghaus, Joseph H. Sharp, and Julius Rolshoven were also members of the SWA. The Society of Western Artists was divided into active, associate, and honorary membership. The purpose of the organization was to bring the work of its members before the public by means of travelling exhibitions. The SWA was disbanded in 1914, but in the following year, when the Taos artists decided to establish their own society, the SWA served as a model for how it could be done.[7]

In 1911, Phillips (in a short history written in the third person) described his long efforts to establish an art colony as follows: "For thirteen years he has held to the hope for an association of artists, who by their various talents and genius, could make complete the record of beauty which no single one could possibly accomplish in a lifetime of endeavor and he has been rewarded by seeing this hope take form until the splendid results of the united efforts, of the 'Taos Colony' for the past few years, predict the ultimate success of his highest ideals."[8]

In August 1914, however, Phillips wrote a letter to his friend Charles A. Cumming in Des Moines, Iowa, that revealed a much less positive attitude about the art colony. Cumming had offered to organize an exhibition of paintings by the Taos artists, but Phillips had to report that there was little interest in doing so. He said that he had spoken with Couse, Sharp, and Blumenschein, and they did not think there was any chance of sales and preferred "to keep their stuff to show to tourists." Phillips went on to say that he was "disappointed over the way some of the men have acted this year, my dreams seem to be about to vanish. I have helped them all in a thousand ways and I hope to keep on but it is getting hard to keep from getting bitter."[9]

Whatever the reasons for the attitudes among the artists observed by Phillips in the summer of 1914, in the following summer the Taos artists were ready to get together to work for their common benefit. Six artists—Joseph H. Sharp, Ernest L. Blumenschein, Bert G. Phillips, Oscar E. Berninghaus, E. Irving Couse, and W. Herbert Dunton—joined together to form the Taos Society of Artists.[10]

Bert Phillips, who was elected secretary, wrote in the minutes that "The first meeting took place at the home of Dr. Martin July 1915." Phillips did not record the exact date in the minutes, but in the same document he referred to the "annual meeting July 15," and whereas all subsequent annual meetings were held in the middle of July, it is a virtual certainty that the first meeting of the Society was held on July 15, 1915. Although the first meeting was at the home of Dr. Thomas P. Martin, it appears that Dr. Martin played no part in the event, and that the meeting was held in the rooms that Oscar Berninghaus was renting from the doctor that summer. Berninghaus's daughter, Dorothy Brandenburg, has stated that this was the case. The fact that Berninghaus was elected temporary chairman at the first meet-

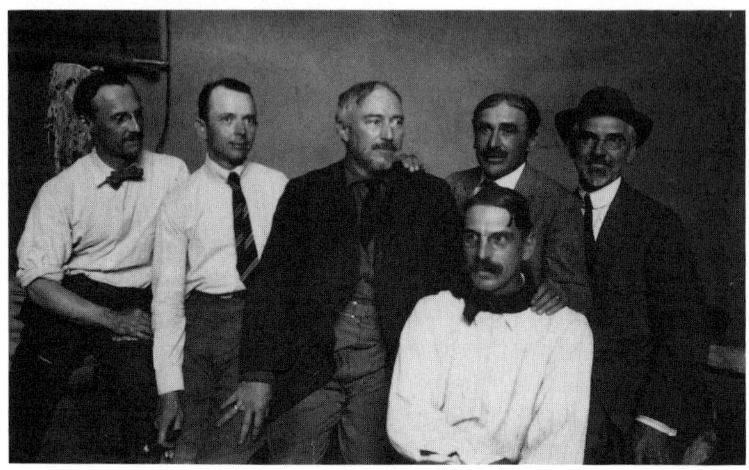

The six founding members of the Taos Society of Artists, circa 1915. From left: Ernest L. Blumenschein, Oscar E. Berninghaus, E. Irving Couse, Bert G. Phillips, and Joseph H. Sharp; in front: W. Herbert Dunton. Courtesy Museum of New Mexico (neg. no. 28820).

ing adds credence to this claim, because Berninghaus would naturally have been given this honor if the meeting were held in his living quarters.[11]

In addition to the lack of an exact date and place, other important things were left unsaid by Phillips in his minutes for the annual meeting of 1915 (and also 1916). Although Blumenschein was listed as a founding member, he was not present at the 1915 meeting, and he likewise did not attend the 1916 annual meeting. When first considering this strange situation, the author assumed that Blumenschein was not in Taos in the summer of 1915, but the *Taos Valley News* for July 6, 1915, reported that he had arrived in town. It is also interesting to note that Walter Ufer and Victor Higgins were in Taos in the summer of 1915. The *Taos Valley News* for July 13, 1915, quoted a Santa Fe news item stating that Ufer was painting at Isleta Pueblo, but that he was going to join former Chicago Mayor Carter H. Harrison in Santa Fe, after which they would both proceed to Taos. The *Taos Valley News* for August 3, 1915, revealed that Blumenschein and Victor Higgins had gone to Hondo Canyon to camp for a week, but the newspaper did not reveal how long Higgins had been in town.

With the above facts in mind, it is possible to propose a hypothetical scenario that might explain why things happened as they did in 1915 and 1916. Since Blumenschein was in Taos in July 1915, his absence from the first meeting of the Society may mean that he was boycotting the meeting. The fact that Ufer and Higgins had made a point of being in Taos in July 1915 may provide an answer for Blumenschein's actions. It is possible that Blumenschein wanted Ufer and Higgins to be charter members of the Taos Society of Artists. If so, he must have proposed to his associates before the founding meeting that Ufer and Higgins be included, but it appears that a majority of the founding members objected that these two had not worked in Taos long enough to prove their long-term interest in the area. The adoption at the founding meeting of the rule that members "must have worked in Taos three years . . ." prevented Ufer and Higgins from becoming members in 1915. Although given only as a brief statement in the minutes of the founding meeting, the three-year rule likely engendered considerable controversy and probably was agreed to by a majority well before the meeting took place. Knowing that he had lost the argument, Blumenschein thus may have refused to attend the first meeting. Blumenschein also did not attend the 1916 annual meeting; it is possible that he boycotted this meeting for the same reason as in

1915. The first meeting that Blumenschein did attend was the special meeting called on the plaza on August 12, 1916. It is important to note that this meeting was called so that Blumenschein could propose a motion that visiting artists be allowed to exhibit with the Society. This motion, which carried, was specifically designed to allow Ufer and Higgins to exhibit with the Society. At another special meeting two days later, the secretary was instructed to invite Ufer and Higgins to send pictures to the Taos Society of Artists exhibition in Santa Fe. These actions led to their admission as active members in 1917, after they had satisfied the three-year rule.

The *Taos Valley News* did not carry any notice of the founding of the Taos Society of Artists. This is highly surprising, because the editor of the newspaper was interested in promoting the art colony, and he habitually printed anything about the Taos artists that was even slightly newsworthy. If the scenario proposed above is true, however, it appears that the Society began in discord. The embarrassing conflict that seems to have arisen regarding the founding meeting may have left the editor of the newspaper at a loss as to what to report.

Blumenschein was at the center of most—but not all—of the controversy in the Society. After Blumenschein's letter regarding range-finder paintings was published in the *American Art News* in September 1918, considerable anger was felt in the art community (this event is covered in detail on pages 32 and 107–11 of this book).[12] One event that Blumenschein did not incite (as far as we know) was the effort by the Society to have the artist Henry Balink deported as an undesirable alien (see the comments on p. 60 about the special meeting of the Society held on October 30, 1919). No further documentary evidence has come to light regarding this incident, but in the past several years the author has spoken with two people who knew Balink, and they were able to illuminate the situation somewhat. They both said that Balink had a high opinion of his own work, and he never hesitated to criticize the work of other artists. It is likely, then, that some of the Taos artists were angered by Balink's comments about their work, considering his remarks to be personal insults rather than artistic criticism.

In some ways the Society reached the peak of its success just after the end of the Great War. Ten paintings were sold from the circuit exhibition in 1919. E. I. Couse, who was still president that year, said at the 1919 annual meeting that "the exhibitions of the Society have become the event of the year in many cities."

In the late spring of 1919, Bert Phillips and Ernest Blumenschein went on a painting trip in New Mexico and Arizona for six weeks in Blumenschein's automobile. Upon their return, Phillips wrote to a friend and repeated Blumenschein's comments that "every 20 years we make a long trip, the first was with a wagon, now this was by auto, and the next is planned for a flying machine, 1939?"[13]

The success and fellowship that marked the early years of the Society eventually faded, however. W. Herbert Dunton's resignation from the TSA was announced at the 1922 annual meeting. Other than the documents in this book (see pages 10, 78, and 93), nothing else has come to light that would explain Dunton's actions or even provide the exact date of his resignation.

In contrast, a great deal more has been learned about the events that led to Blumenschein's forced resignation in the summer of 1923 (see pages 84–89). On May 26, 1923, Blumenschein, Higgins, and Ufer nominated Jozef Bakos and William P. Henderson for membership in the Taos Society of Artists. However, Bakos and Henderson apparently found little support among the other members of the Society. Eleven days later (June 6), Blumenschein, Higgins, and Ufer went to Santa Fe and joined with Bakos and Henderson, as well as Frank Applegate, Gustave Baumann, and B. J. O. Nordfeldt, to form an organization they

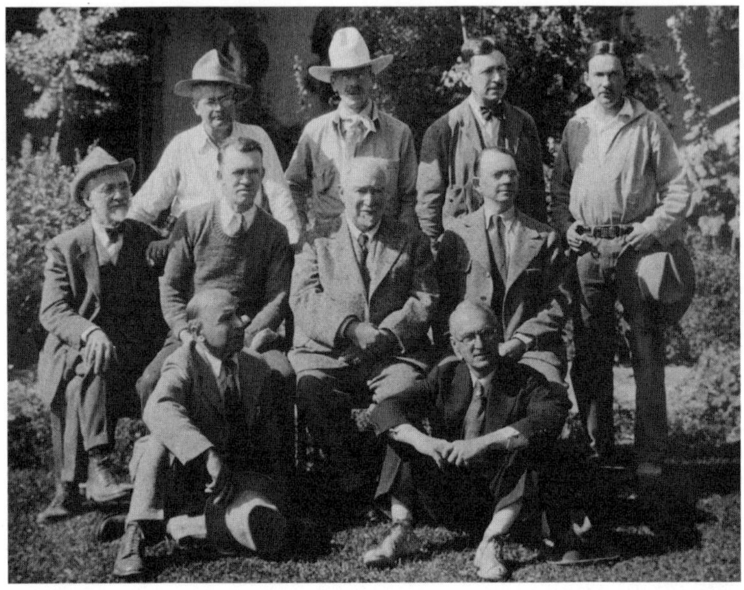

A third photograph of ten former members of the Taos Society of Artists in the garden of E. I. Couse in Taos in the summer of 1932 (also see photos on pages 53 and 54). Standing left to right: Walter Ufer, W. Herbert Dunton, Victor Higgins, Kenneth Adams. Seated left to right: Joseph H. Sharp, E. Martin Hennings, E. Irving Couse, Oścar E. Berninghaus. Sitting on the ground: Bert G. Phillips and Ernest L. Blumenschein. Courtesy Kit Carson Historic Museums, Taos. Photo by C. E. Lord.

named the New Mexico Painters. Blumenschein, the driving force behind this new society, was named its first secretary. These eight artists, who considered themselves to be the avant-garde of art in New Mexico, had founded an organization that was a direct competitor of the Taos Society of Artists, and it was for this reason that the 1923 meetings of the Taos Society became so acrimonious. A change made in the Constitution and By-Laws of the Taos Society required Blumenschein to either serve as secretary for the 1923–24 season or resign from the Taos Society, "unless there be a reason acceptable to the Society." His reply that he was already the secretary of the New Mexico Painters and could not do both jobs was not accepted by the Taos Society, and he was therefore forced to resign.[14]

The Taos Society of Artists sponsored a circuit exhibition at least until the middle of 1926 (an announcement was made at the annual meeting in July 1926 that the exhibition was in Denver). The New Mexico Painters had a circuit exhibition as late as the spring of 1927; Ufer visited the exhibition in Chicago and wrote a letter to Blumenschein on April 5 describing it to him. Ufer said in his letter that he was going to "continue to stay out of their [the New Mexico Painters] exhibitions—also the Taos Society of Artists." His decision to refrain from exhibiting with both organizations grew out of his conviction that it did not benefit his career to exhibit with a group when he could get all the one-man shows that he wanted. Furthermore, he complained to Blumenschein that their work did not "hang well" in a group show because of the many different styles, sizes, mediums, and prices. In essence, then, Ufer was saying that these two organizations were no longer providing him with benefits that would justify any effort on his part to remain a member. Some of the other artists must have felt the same way by that time.[15]

In writing about the Taos Society of Artists in 1951, Kenneth Adams stated that "a quorum of its members met at the home of Bert G. Phillips one night in March, 1927, and by a unanimous vote ended the existence of the Taos Society of Artists" (see page 12). However, Ufer's April 5, 1927, letter to Blumenschein referred to the Taos Society as if it were still in existence. This seeming inconsistency can be added to the bigger question of how a quorum could be gathered in late winter in Taos when most of the artists were habitually out of town. Writing 24 years after the fact, did Adams remember correctly? The *Taos Valley News,* usually such a good source of information on the artists, does not help here, because practically none of the issues for 1927 have survived. Until other documents come to light to either confirm or refute the date given by Adams, though, we will have to assume that a cold night in March 1927 marked the end of the Taos Society of Artists.[16]

In the early years of the Taos art colony, Bert Phillips urged artists to come to Taos to paint, reportedly saying, "There is a lifetime's work here for twenty men." His statement could now be paraphrased, "There is a lifetime's work for twenty art historians." Much has been done to sort out the facts about the early Taos artists, but a great deal of work remains to be done. The incentive is that the facts are always much more interesting (and useful) than the legends.

The records of the Taos Society of Artists are at the Fray Angélico Chávez History Library of the Museum of New Mexico in Santa Fe. The documents, contained in Box 141, Manuscripts Collection, include the Constitution and By-Laws, minutes of the meetings, reports of the secretary, a few financial records, and miscellaneous correspondence. Also included are two years of business correspondence, a number of catalogs, and Paul A. F. Walter's file of correspondence with artists that dates from his tenure as associate director of the Museum of New Mexico.

Most of the material in the Taos Society of Artists file has been included in this book, except that the business correspondence, exhibition catalogs, and Paul Walter's correspondence have been included only in occasional notes. Every effort has been made to retain the wording and punctuation of the original documents, in accordance with the belief that the manner in which a document is written tells something about the writer. Editing changes generally have been restricted to correcting typographical and spelling errors and to standardizing capitalization. Punctuation was changed only when the original style might cause confusion. Where the original was illegible or a word was apparently left out by mistake, words or phrases were added in brackets when the intended meaning seemed clear; ellipsis points were used when there was uncertainty about the meaning. In a few instances, explanatory notes have been added in brackets to furnish additional information or to provide headings where none existed. Otherwise, all headings are printed as they appeared in the original.

Robert Rankin White
May 1998
Albuquerque, New Mexico

Notes

1. Laura Bickerstaff, *Pioneer Artists of Taos* (Denver: Old West Publishing Co., 1983) (revision of 1955 edition), p. 29.

2. Blumenschein's statement that Sharp told him about Taos in 1896 was contained in an article written for the *New Mexico State Tribune* and published in that Albuquerque newspaper on May 10, 1926. The headline for the article (which appeared on page 1) was: "Conversation in France led to Establishment of Taos Artists' Colony by World Weary Painters." This article was also published in *El Palacio* 20 (no. 10), May 15, 1926.

Information from the records of the Académie Julian are from Catherine Fehrer, *The Julian Academy* (New York: Shepherd Gallery,

1989) as listed in Virginia Couse Leavitt, *Eanger Irving Couse: Image Maker for America* (Albuquerque: The Albuquerque Museum, 1991), p. 46.

The Académie Julian still exists, although greatly altered in structure. In 1968, the school was reorganized by the artist Guillaume Met de Penninghen as the École Superieure d'Art Graphique (ESAG). ESAG is the official name of the school, although Académie Julian is used as an overall designation, but when students are asked where they attend school, the reply would most likely be "the Penninghen."

3. Blumenschein papers, Archives of American Art, Smithsonian Institution, microfilm roll 270, frame 167. This information is from notes written in Blumenschein's hand; although some of the dates in this material are problematical, the dates he gives for his first western trips seem to be correct.

4. Some years ago I humorously began referring to the place at which the wagon wheel broke as the "Sacred Site." I began looking for the Sacred Site in 1990, and on July 16, 1993, some friends and I finally found it near the community of Lama. The search was described in detail in Robert R. White, "Sacred Site," *Southwest Art* 23 (No. 12, May 1994): pp. 60–66, 100.

5. Julie Schimmel and Robert R. White, *Bert Geer Phillips and the Taos Art Colony* (Albuquerque: University of New Mexico Press, 1994) pp. 41–42. This book covers Phillips's first few years in Taos in great detail.

6. Schimmel and White, *Bert Geer Phillips and the Taos Art Colony*, pp. 65, 290.

7. The March 14, 1901, issue of *The Taos Cresset* revealed that Phillips had been invited to exhibit with the Society of Western Artists in Chicago. Typically, a candidate for membership was invited to exhibit with the SWA and then was either accepted or rejected by a vote of the members in the following year. The January 16, 1902, issue of *The Taos Cresset* stated that Phillips had been elected a member of the SWA. For further information on the Society of Western Artists, see Schimmel and White, *Bert Geer Phillips and the Taos Art Colony*, pp. 67–68. Also see Virginia Couse Leavitt, *Eanger Irving Couse: Image Maker for America*, (Albuquerque: The Albuquerque Museum, 1991): pp. 27–28. Leavitt also describes another prototype for the Taos Society of Artists, known

as The Society of Men Who Paint the Far West; E. I. Couse and E. L. Blumenschein were members of this society, which was formed in 1912.

8. Schimmel and White, *Bert Geer Phillips and the Taos Art Colony*, pp. 68, 321.

9. Bert G. Phillips to Charles A. Cumming, August 7, 1914, Charles Atherton Cumming Papers, 1902–1928. Ms 331. Rio Grande Historical Collections, New Mexico State University Library.

10. It is interesting to speculate that if Frank Paul Sauerwein had lived, he might have been the seventh founding member of the Taos Society of Artists. He bought a house in Taos (now part of the Taos Inn) in 1906 and became a respected member of the art colony. He contracted tuberculosis, however, and died in 1910 while visiting in Connecticut. See Elaine Maher Harrison, "Frank Paul Sauerwein," *Panhandle-Plains Historical Review* 33 (1960): pp. 1–68 and Michael R. Grauer, "Frank Paul Sauerwein," *Southwest Art* (July 1996): pp. 82–86.

11. Dorothy Brandenburg (Berninghaus's daughter) told Virginia Couse Leavitt, who told the author, that the first meeting was held in Berninghaus's rooms; the author subsequently discussed this with Mrs. Brandenburg on December 12, 1990. The *Taos Valley News* for June 29, 1915, noted that Berninghaus and his children had arrived in Taos and were "staying at the home of Dr. T. P. Martin."

12. For further information on range-finder paintings, see Robert R. White, "Ernest Blumenschein and the Great War," *Ayer y Hoy en Taos* (Journal of the Taos County Historical Society) (Winter 1986): pp. 3–6.

13. Bert G. Phillips to Charles A. Cumming, July 13, 1919, Charles Atherton Cumming Papers, 1902–1928. Ms 331. Rio Grande Historical Collections, New Mexico State University Library.

14. Details about this crisis may be found in Robert R. White, "The New Mexico Painters, 1923–1926," *Southwest Art* 15 (no. 2, May 1986): pp. 76–81.

15. Letter from Walter Ufer (in Chicago) to Ernest L. Blumenschein (probably in Taos), dated April 5, 1927. Blumenschein Family Papers, courtesy of Elizabeth Cunningham and Skip Miller.

16. The author has benefited from several discussions on this subject with Virginia Couse Leavitt and Suzan Campbell.

1

Introduction

Beginning in 1898, artists began to settle in the northern New Mexico community of Taos. Some of these artists were essentially self-taught, but most had extensive academic training, including years of study in Europe. They came from diverse backgrounds and never formed a school of painting, but they all felt the need to develop a truly American form of art. What attracted them to Taos, and then kept them there to form a major American art colony, were the crystal-clear sky and brilliant sunshine, the glorious landscape, and a unique blend of cultures that provided unlimited pictorial possibilities.

Joseph Henry Sharp, usually considered the father of the Taos art colony, first visited there in 1893. Sharp had a lifelong interest in Indians, and his Indian paintings are known for their anthropological accuracy. Beginning in 1902, Sharp spent a few months of each year in Taos, but he concentrated his efforts on painting the Plains Indians in Montana, feeling that the culture of the Plains Indians would disappear before that of the Pueblo Indians. Sharp established permanent residence in Taos in 1912, although for years he travelled, and painted, around the world.

While J. H. Sharp was in Paris in 1895, he told two fellow art students, Ernest L. Blumenschein and Bert G. Phillips, about the beauty of the Taos area. In 1898, Blumenschein and Phillips decided to take a sketching tour of the West. In May they purchased a wagon and team in Denver with the intention of going to Mexico, but a broken wagon wheel in northern New Mexico in September caused a change in plans. Just by chance, Taos was the closest town where the wheel could be repaired, and in a coin toss it fell to Blumenschein to take the wheel there on horseback. It was a slow journey and Blumenschein had time to observe the beautiful New Mexico autumn. When he returned with the repaired wheel, both artists agreed to end their travel in Taos. After three months, Phillips had decided to stay, and he became the first artist to make his permanent residence in Taos, but Blumenschein returned to New York and was to spend most of the next decade in France. Beginning in 1910, Blumenschein spent every summer in Taos, and in 1919 his family settled there.

In 1899, Oscar E. Berninghaus rode into northern New Mexico on the Denver & Rio Grande Railroad in the course of completing a series of sketches for the railroad. The train crew told him about the community of Taos, located at the base of a mountain off to the east. Berninghaus went to Taos, and although he stayed only a week, he was fascinated by the place. He returned to his home in St. Louis and worked hard to develop his professional reputation there, but he began spending part of every year in Taos and made it his permanent residence in 1925.

E. Irving Couse first visited Taos in 1902. He had studied and worked in France for many years, but in the 1890s he lived for a time in Washington and had an opportunity to paint the Indians of the area. In the spring of 1902, Ernest Blumenschein suggested to Couse that he go to Taos to paint. When Couse visited Taos, he found everything he wanted in the way of artistic inspiration. He spent the rest of his life painting the Taos Indians.

W. Herbert (Buck) Dunton enrolled in Ernest Blumenschein's class at the Art Students League in New York in 1912, and when Blumenschein went to Taos that summer, he suggested that Dunton would benefit from a summer's work there. As with the artists who had preceded him, Dunton knew as soon as he saw Taos that this was where he wanted to paint and live. Unlike the other artists, however, Dunton usually painted western cowboy scenes; he rarely painted Indians.

These six artists—Sharp, Blumenschein, Phillips, Berninghaus, Couse, and Dunton—formed the Taos Society of Artists in 1915. The primary purpose of the organization was to sell their work through travelling exhibitions (art galleries did not exist in Taos at that time). The success of the Society was immediate and brought critical recognition for the artists and fame to the town in which they lived. In the following years, the Society increased in size with the addition of other artists who had been attracted by the growing reputation of the Taos Society of Artists and who had been inspired by a unique and beautiful country.

The files of the Taos Society of Artists (T.S.A.) have been at the Museum of New Mexico in Santa Fe for many years, first at the Fine Arts Museum and later in the manuscripts collection at the History Library. It is difficult to understand why the existence of this material has remained such a secret. A few archivists, art historians, and art dealers have known of the T.S.A. records and have made some use of them, but the art world at large has been unaware of the treasure that was on file at the Museum.

The Taos Society of Artists files are important because they give a detailed description of the activities of the Society during its entire existence. Where once dates and events could only be guessed at, the files of the Society often provide the correct year and day, and sometimes even the exact hour. Also of importance is the fact that this represents a large collection of material that is written in the words of the Taos artists themselves. As such, it provides a rare glimpse into the personal lives of these artists, revealing their hopes and plans, the financial difficulties they faced, and finally, the conflicts that invariably arise in any organization.

The first meeting of the Taos Society of Artists was held in July 1915. For many years it was assumed that the Taos Society of Artists was formed in 1912. The origin of the 1912 date seems to have been Van Deren Coke's *Taos and Santa Fe,* and because the publication of this book in 1963 coincided with the rise in interest in the early Taos artists (or more properly, helped to initiate that interest), and because it became the standard work on the subject, this date was accepted without question.[1] This is not to say that there was no conflicting testimony. Laura Bickerstaff, in her 1955 book *Pioneer Artists of Taos,* stated almost as an afterthought that the Taos Society of Artists had been "chartered" in 1916.[2] During the early 1930s, many of the artists who had been in the Society were interviewed by Blanche Grant while she was writing her history of Taos entitled *When Old Trails Were New;* in her chapter on the Taos art colony, she said that the Society had been formed in 1914.[3] The first reference to the 1915 date was in an article by Ernest L. Blumenschein for the September 1917 issue of *The American Magazine of Art,* in which it was stated that "two years ago the Art Society was formed."[4] The 1915 date also was published in Patricia Janis Broder's book *Taos: A Painter's Dream;* Broder had access to copies of the T.S.A. records and made some use of them.[5]

Thus, four dates have been published as the year of formation of the Taos Society of Artists: 1912, 1914, 1915, and 1916. However, records at the Museum of New Mexico clearly establish 1915 as the correct date; the other dates given can easily be explained as a result of the imperfect memories of artists who were asked years later to remember how it all began. It has been suggested that there was an informal meeting of the Taos Society of Artists in 1912,[6] but no corroborating documentary evidence has been found.

Considerable controversy has arisen as well over how many artists were members of the Taos Society of Artists. The Society has been spoken of in terms of "the six," "the eight," "the ten," and in recent years, "the eleven." Laura Bickerstaff was only interested in the six founding members—Berninghaus, Blumenschein, Couse, Dunton, Phillips, and Sharp—although, ironically, she hardly discussed the Society and concentrated on the theme that these six were the pioneer founders of the art colony. She reluctantly allowed Blumenschein, in his introduction to *Pioneer Artists of Taos,* to discuss Ufer and Higgins, and later writers often described the T.S.A. in terms of these eight artists.[7] Van Deren Coke's *Taos and Santa Fe* featured a photograph of the "Taos Society of Artists, 1927," adding Hennings and Adams to the first eight, for a total of ten.[8] This number and this photograph became definitive, and they were the basis for a successful advertising campaign by a major Santa Fe gallery during the 1970s. Two books published in 1980 on the Taos Society of Artists, Mary Carroll Nelson's *Legendary Artists of Taos* and Patricia Janis Broder's *Taos: A Painter's Dream,* described the Society in terms of eleven members, adding Catharine Carter Critcher to the list.[9]

But again, the files of the Society at the Museum of New Mexico reveal the complete history of membership: there were twenty-one members in three categories—active, associate, and honorary. The eleven artists previously mentioned were active members, as was Julius Rolshoven, who was elected an associate member in 1917, made an active member in 1918, and was returned to associate status in 1923. The other associate members were Robert Henri, Albert Groll, John Sloan, Randall Davey, B. J. O. Nordfeldt, Birger Sandzen, and Gustave Baumann. The list is impressive. Included among the associates are some of the major figures in twentieth century American art. The only two honorary members were Edgar Lee Hewett and Frank Springer.

It certainly can be argued that the active members who were in the "group of ten" were the core of the Society and brought fame both to the Taos Society of Artists and the community of Taos. These were the artists who settled in Taos and lived there long after the Society was just a memory. There is some justification for adding Catharine Critcher to the list, as she was elected an active member in 1924. If Critcher is included, however, Julius Rolshoven certainly must be added as well, because he was an active member for five years and had an important place in the life of the art colony while he was in Taos. This is not a plea for the establishment of another sacred number—the twelve—although it should be borne in mind that this was indeed the number of active members in the Taos Society of Artists. Rather, it is an effort to affirm that there were twenty-one members of the Taos Society of Artists and each played a part, however minor, in the history of the Society.

The concept of the Taos Society of Artists as ten men, however, has taken hold of the public imagination. In the absence of documents on the Society, visual evidence of this group of ten artists existed in the photograph published in Coke's *Taos and Santa Fe.*

The photograph of the ten men, which is usually described

as the Taos Society of Artists in 1927, deserves further mention. Rarely has a photograph played so large a role in determining the way in which the history of people, places, and events is perceived. Actually, three photos were taken on the same day, but with the artists in different positions (see illustrations pp. xxiv, 53–54). To be historically correct, the three photographs cannot be said to be pictures of the Taos Society of Artists, and the evidence is irrefutable that the photos were not taken in 1927. The presence of Hennings and Adams in the photographs is the key to refuting the 1927 date. Adams was not elected a member until July 1926, so the photographs probably would not have been taken before then, but Hennings was not in Taos at any time during 1926 or 1927. Martin Hennings left Taos at Christmas 1925 because of the illness of his mother, and remained in Chicago until his marriage on July 20, 1926. He and his wife then left immediately for Europe and stayed there for sixteen months, returning to Chicago in November 1927. They did not move to Taos until early 1928, so the earliest the photographs could have been taken was the spring of 1928.[10]

The first known use of one of the photographs of the ten artists was in the first edition of Blanche Grant's *When Old Trails Were New,* published in 1934.[11] The photograph was identified simply as "Group of Taos Artists." The photo was taken by C. E. Lord, who took many of the other photos in the book.[12] It is quite possible that Lord took the photo of the ten artists at Miss Grant's request for inclusion in her book. If so, this would mean that the photographs probably were taken in 1932 or 1933. A proof of one of these photographs in the photo archives at the Museum of New Mexico has a note on the back in an unknown hand that the photo was "Taken in yard of E. I. Couse in summer 1932." This would seem to settle the question.

To be precise, the photographs of the ten artists can be said to represent nothing more than a portrait of those former members of the Taos Society of Artists who had the foresight to be in Taos on the day that the photos were taken. As stated above, the Taos Society of Artists no longer existed when these photographs were taken. Even if the photos had been taken in 1927, there would still be a problem in describing the group as members of the Taos Society of Artists, because Dunton resigned in 1922 and Blumenschein resigned in 1923. In the final analysis, though, none of this detracts from the importance of these three photographs; they are the best pictures that we have of the active members of the Taos Society of Artists. No other picture has been found that includes so many of the artists who were responsible for establishing the fame of the Society.

The earliest document in the Taos Society of Artists files is a handwritten copy of the minutes of the founding meeting, held in July 1915. The minutes of the 1915 meeting appear to have been written months afterwards, as the secretary, Bert Phillips, could not remember the exact date and left room to insert the day of the month at a later time (the meeting probably was held on July 15 because those first minutes contain a reference to future annual meetings to be held on July 15). It is likely that the minutes for 1915 were written just before the 1916 meeting; minutes for the meetings of both years were written in a booklet purchased for that purpose. In later years (particularly when Walter Ufer was secretary), the minutes were sometimes prepared in final form only after they had been read and approved at the following annual meeting, thus explaining why the minutes often contain comments about events that occurred some months after the meeting.

The 1915 meeting was held at the home of a local doctor, T. P. Martin, but most subsequent meetings were held in the studio of one of the members (often in the studio of the current Society president). At least one meeting (August 12, 1916) was held at the plaza in Taos. The annual meetings were always held in mid-summer, because some of the members did not stay in Taos during the winter. In addition to the annual meeting, special meetings were sometimes held in late summer or early autumn when problems arose that were of concern to the membership.

The files of the Society contain some surprises, such as the special meeting called on October 30, 1919, at which all members present voted to draft a letter requesting the deportation of fellow artist Henry Balink. Seemingly even more out of character was a meeting on August 8, 1920, at which they discussed the merits of placing a sign on the Taos plaza stating that "the Taos Society of Artists does not approve of soliciting but would be glad to receive visitors and show their works upon request and after four P.M." The matter was dropped after considerable discussion.

The most amusing event in the history of the Taos Society of Artists certainly must have been the dance given by the Society on the night of July 27, 1921. Those who paid to attend the dance were led to believe that their ticket entitled them to a chance at a painting to be raffled during the evening. Instead of a painting, however, the prize the Society planned to give was "a certain decrepit, maimed and forlorn dog-about-town." As it turned out, though, a pig was substituted for the dog due to "the dog's physical condition and also to his viciousness"; the financial report on the dance included the expenditure of 70¢ on "decorations for pig." The cooperation and fellowship evidenced at the dance in 1921, however, were soon to fade.

At some time before the 1922 annual meeting, W. Herbert Dunton resigned from the Taos Society of Artists, thereby giving a hint of problems that were to threaten the existence of the Society in the following year. The files of the Society furnish two possible explanations for Dunton's resignation. In a letter written by Blumenschein on July 15, 1922 (included in the T.S.A. records for 1922), he repeated Dunton's statement that "his reason for resigning was because he did not care to belong to a society in which the sec'y [Ufer] referred to the president [Blumenschein] as a 'bald-headed S.B.'" In the minutes of the 1924 annual meeting, at which Dunton's name was submitted for re-election and then withdrawn, the comment was made that Dunton had originally resigned because he would not accept his obligation to serve as the secretary of the Society.

Serving as secretary was a task so burdensome and time-consuming that most of the members demonstrated a reluctance to undertake the position. It fell to the secretary to arrange and manage the exhibition circuit and to carry on the voluminous correspondence of the Society. The extent of the task can be judged by reading the secretary's report for 1920, in which Berninghaus stated that he received 129 letters and wrote 141 in reply, "including 53 letters to individuals calling attention to the exhibition."

The problem of who would be secretary was the issue that precipitated a disastrous sequence of events in 1923. At the annual meeting on July 13, J. H. Sharp was elected president, but "after repeated balloting the office of secretary for the ensuing year brought no definite result." Deciding to postpone this matter, consideration was then given to membership nominations for Sheldon Parsons, Theodore Van Solen, and E. Martin Hennings. None of the three was elected; however, Hennings was elected unanimously in the following year; thus the negative response seems to have been a reflection of the general dissatisfaction at the proceedings. After this stalemate in the vote, Sharp declared his refusal to accept the presidency, and the meeting was adjourned for ten days. At the meeting on July 23, the membership accepted Couse's proposed change in the Constitution whereby one officer in the Society would conduct its business. The change required that "each active member shall serve in alphabetical order for one year and that a refusal to serve be considered equivalent to a resignation from the Society unless there be a reason acceptable to the Society." When Blumenschein was informed that the obligation was his, he wrote a letter stating why he could not undertake the duties that year. At a meeting on July 31, Blumenschein's excuse "became a matter of lengthy and at times heated discussion." Ufer finally stormed out in protest, whereupon a majority of the five remaining members voted to reject Blumenschein's excuse, thus forcing him to resign from the Society.

Blumenschein seems to have been poorly treated in this matter because he had a valid excuse and apparently indicated his willingness to serve in the following year. In 1924, Higgins and then Phillips offered vague claims of illness and were excused from serving as the officer of the Society. Perhaps Blumenschein's troubles stemmed in part from the angry letter he wrote in the summer of 1922 after his term as president had ended, in which he expressed his dissatisfaction with the Society (see his letter of July 15, included with the records for 1922).

After reading of the Society's difficulties concerning the secretaryship, one must wonder why the artists did not designate the secretary as a nonmember and hire someone to do the job for them. Another possibility would have been for a family member of one of the artists to serve as secretary.

During its final years, little controversy occurred in the Society. At the annual meetings, as had been done many times before, the secretary might repeat comments from dealers that the prices of paintings were too high, and then urge all members to send their best work on the circuit.

The Taos Society of Artists disbanded in 1927. No records from that year exist in the archives of the Museum of New Mexico, probably because no one felt the need to record the demise of the organization, but Kenneth Adams was later to write that " . . . a quorum of its members met at the home of Bert G. Phillips one night in March, 1927, and by a unanimous vote ended the existence of the Taos Society of Artists."[13]

It is often said that the Taos Society of Artists dissolved because it became too successful, that the work of these artists was so popular that they could not keep up with their other work and continue the circuit. This may be true for some of the artists, but this is not the impression that one has after reading the records of the Society. It seems that for most of its members, the Society had outlived its usefulness and maintaining it had become a burden. It also appears that the circuit had ceased to provide the sales and the publicity that would justify the work required.

Confirmation of this last statement, and some tantalizing comments on the last days of the Taos Society of Artists, appeared in print in autumn 1927:

> At any rate, the acknowledged masters formed some years back an academy called The Taos Society. But now the Society can hardly claim to have the greatest of the Taos artists on its roster. Three of the younger artists—younger in spirit, if not in years—have recently withdrawn from the Society. "I was ready to tell them my reasons," one of the recusants related with wry amusement, "but the motion

to accept my resignation came so promptly it seemed unnecessary to say anything further." The New York exhibitions of the Taos Society once attracted much attention, but the last two or three, it is said, have failed to get satisfactory recognition from critics or purchasers.[14]

Who these three "younger artists" were is not revealed, but a strong suggestion emerges that the Society ended in discord and not in the warmth of mutual admiration and professional success.

However the end came, it does not dim the glory of earlier years, of that time when Berninghaus could justifiably state that "the Society is undoubtedly one of the best known in the United States." From before World War I until the mid-1920s, hardly an issue of *El Palacio* appeared that did not contain a reproduction of a painting by one of the Taos artists, mention of the artists' activities, or the news of the sale of a major work by one of them. So much importance was placed upon the T.S.A. that when the Society opened an exhibition of paintings at the Museum of New Mexico in 1918, *El Palacio* devoted eight pages to reporting the event.[15] In the final analysis, the extraordinary interest in the Taos Society of Artists at the present time is sufficient testimony to the contributions of these artists to American art.

It is most fortunate that the records of the Taos Society of Artists have been preserved. The fact that they were preserved, and further, that they were carefully assembled through the years during which the Society existed, tells a great deal about the seriousness and professionalism of these artists. It is no surprise that during a trip in 1925, Joseph Sharp wrote to another T.S.A. member in Taos with the comment, "File the enclosed with the archives!" These were people who understood their place in history.

The members of the Taos Society of Artists as listed in the records of the Society were as follows:

1. Joseph H. Sharp : active member (charter), July 1915.
2. Ernest L. Blumenschein : active member (charter), July 1915; resigned July 31, 1923.
3. Bert G. Phillips : active member (charter), July 1915.
4. Oscar E. Berninghaus : active member (charter), July 1915.
5. E. Irving Couse : active member (charter), July 1915.
6. W. Herbert Dunton : active member (charter), July 1915; resigned in 1922.
7. Walter Ufer : active member, elected July 15, 1917.
8. Victor Higgins : active member, elected July 15, 1917.
9. Julius Rolshoven : elected associate member on July 15, 1917; elected active member on July 16, 1918; returned to associate status on July 23, 1923.
10. Robert Henri : associate member, elected July 16, 1918.
11. Edgar L. Hewett : honorary member, elected August 26, 1918.
12. Frank Springer : honorary member, elected August 26, 1918.
13. Albert Groll : associate member, elected July 11, 1919.
14. John Sloan : associate member, elected July 12, 1921.
15. Randall Davey : associate member, elected July 12, 1921.
16. B. J. O. Nordfeldt : associate member, elected July 12, 1921.
17. Birger Sandzen : associate member, elected July 12, 1922.
18. Gustave Baumann : associate member, elected July 12, 1922.

19. Catharine C. Critcher : active member, elected July 12, 1924.
20. E. Martin Hennings : active member, elected July 12, 1924.
21. Kenneth Adams : active member, elected July 12, 1926.

2

Constitution and By-Laws

The Taos Society of Artists

Constitution and By-Laws
[Adopted on August 26, 1918]

Article I

The name of this Society shall be "The Taos Society of Artists."

Article II

The location of the Society shall be Taos, State of New Mexico.

Article III

This Society is formed for educational purposes, to develop a high standard of art among its members, and to aid in the diffusion of taste for art in general. To promote and stimulate the practical expressions of art—to preserve and promote the native art.

To facilitate bringing before the public through exhibitions and other means tangible results of the work of its members. To promote, maintain and preserve high standards of artistic excellence in painting, and to encourage sculpture, architecture, applied arts, music, literature, ethnology and archaeology solely as it pertains to New Mexico and the States adjoining.

Article IV

The business and the affairs of the Society shall be conducted by a Governing Board, which shall consist of the president, secretary, treasurer and one active member, who shall be chosen by ballot by the active members of the Society at the regular annual meeting.

Article V

The officers of the Society shall be a president, secretary, treasurer and the member of the Governing Board. They shall be elected by the active members present at the regular annual meeting of the Society, and shall serve for one year, or until their successors are elected and qualify. Vacancies in any office shall be filled by the Governing Board. The duties of the officers shall be such as usually attach thereto, and as may be prescribed by the By-Laws.

Article VI

The membership of the Society is to be determined and classified in such manner as the By-Laws may prescribe. Only active members shall have a vote on any of the business or affairs of the Society.

Article VII

No indebtedness shall be incurred for any amount exceeding the unappropriated funds in the possession of the secretary-treasurer, except by authority of the Governing Board.

Article VIII

The Constitution or By-Laws may be changed or amended at any annual meeting of the Society by a majority vote of the active members present, provided that notice in writing of proposed change or amendment be sent, together with the secretary's notice of the meeting.

Taos Society of Artists
By-Laws

1. The membership of the Society shall be divided into the following classes, viz: Active, Associate and Honorary.

2. Active members shall be those whose accomplishments and standing in the Art of Painting have won for them jury recognition in some exhibition which the Society considers standard and representative, and who have practiced their artistic vocation in Taos, New Mexico, or immediate vicinity for a period of three years or a part of three separate years, provided each part thereof be no less than three months, and who otherwise comply with Article III of the Constitution.

3. Associate members shall be those who qualify the same as active members excepting they do not practice their artistic vocation in Taos, New Mexico, or immediate vicinity, but in New Mexico or adjoining States for a period not less than three years or a part of three separate years, providing each part thereof be not less than three months.

4. A vote of two-thirds of the active members of the Society shall constitute election to active or associate membership.

5. Honorary members shall be those who are closely identified with the progress of the Arts and Sciences pertaining

to the Southwest, and who shall be approved by a unanimous vote of the active members present at the regular annual meeting of the Society.

6. Nominations for active, associate and honorary membership must be submitted in writing by at least two active members to the Governing Board at least ten days before the regular annual meeting, and announcement be made of the nomination in the secretary's notice of the meeting.

7. The dues of active and associate members shall be five dollars payable annually on the date of the annual meeting of the Society.

8. Any member failing to pay dues or any debt of the Society for six months after the dues have accrued or the debt has been incurred may be dropped from membership.

9. The president shall appoint such committees to serve for a specific purpose as he may deem appropriate.

10. The president of the Society shall be ex-officio a member of every committee.

11. The annual meeting of the Society, for the election of officers, member of the Governing Board, and election of new members shall be held during the second week in July of each year, and five days notice of the meeting shall be given in writing to each member. If for any reason the election is not then held it shall be a continuing duty to hold such election at the first meeting of the Society thereafter. Voting shall be by ballot.

12. Special meetings may be called at any time by the president, or by a written request of two active members. Active members to be notified of meetings three days in advance. A

majority of the active members shall constitute a quorum for business purposes at any annual or special meeting.

13. The Governing Board shall have the power to make rules for the conduct of business affairs and meetings of the Society not inconsistent with the Constitution and By-Laws. All voting for officers and election of members shall be by ballot.

14. All active and associate members shall deem it a special obligation to be represented in all special and circuit exhibitions.

[The Constitution and By-Laws of the Society were subsequently amended as follows:]

July 11, 1919
The membership of the Society shall consist of American citizens and divided into the following classes: viz: Active, Associate and Honorary.

July 23, 1923
There shall be one officer in the Taos Society of Artists whose duty it shall be to conduct the business of the Society. Each active member shall serve in alphabetical order for one year and that a refusal to serve be considered equivalent to a resignation from the Society unless there be a reason acceptable to the Society.

July 23, 1923
Any active member absenting himself for one year and ceasing active participation in the Society shall be classed to associate membership but automatically is reinstated upon his return to qualifications of active membership.

3

Minutes of the Meetings and Related Documents

1915

Minutes of the Taos Society of Artists
[1915 Annual Meeting]

The first meeting took place at the home of Dr. Martin July 1915.[1] Mr. Berninghaus was elected temporary chairman. Mr. E. I. Couse was elected president and B. G. Phillips was elected treasurer & secretary. The members present were Mr. E. I. Couse, Mr. J. H. Sharp, Mr. O. E. Berninghaus, Mr. W. H. Dunton & Mr. B. G. Phillips. Mr. E. L. Blumenschein was absent. The name of the organization was discussed and "Taos Society of Artists" was selected. By unamimous vote it was decided that applicants for membership in the Society must be proposed by two regular members. Such applicants must have worked in Taos three years or at least a part of three different years and have been exhibitors in some representative American art exhibition. Further, applicants must receive the unanimous vote of the members at their annual meeting July 15. The annual dues were fixed at 1.00. Suitable stationery was agreed upon and Mr. O. E. Berninghaus was appointed a committee of one to select same.

1916

Minutes 1915–16
[Second Annual Meeting]

The second annual meeting of The Taos Society of Artists was held in the studio of Mr. O. E. Berninghaus July 15th 1916. Minutes read and approved on motion of the president. All members except Mr. E. L. Blumenschein were present. Secretary was notified to write Mr. W. H. Simpson relative to having pictures of Mr. Berninghaus and Mr. Blumenschein incorporated in the Santa Fe Ry. illustrated lectures.[2] Secretary was also notified to write Mr. McGinnis of Boulder of the acceptance of his proposition to exhibit in Boulder.

Meeting was adjourned on motion of the president, seconded by Mr. Berninghaus.

Special Meeting called on Plaza Aug. 12th.

Mr. Couse presided. Motion by Mr. Blumenschein that majority of vote be necessary to invite a visiting artist to exhibit with the Taos Society of Artists. Seconded by Mr. Dunton. Motion carried. Meeting adjourned until Aug. 14.

Special Meeting of Aug. 14

Called to order by pres. Informal discussion as to merits of amateur artists. On motion of Mr. Blumenschein, seconded by Mr. Dunton, vote was taken as whether amateur artists should be invited to exhibit in Santa Fe. Motion lost.

Secretary was instructed to answer letter for State Fair offering Santa Fe exhibit under certain conditions mentioned. Sec. instructed to have carpenter box pictures for Santa Fe exhibit. To invite Mr. Ufer to send pictures to Santa Fe exhibit.[3] To notify Mr. Higgins.

1917

Secretary's Report for 1916–17

During the past year the Taos Society of Artists have exhibited in Boulder, Colo., Santa Fe, and Las Vegas, N.M., and a special exhibit under the management of Mr. [name omitted] made a circuit of several southern and middle western cities. The Federation of American Art included a group of our pictures in one of their circuits which was out for about a year. There was considerable correspondence with the State Fair Association of New Mexico in regard to an exhibition but as our terms were not accepted the matter fell through. Also after considerable correspondence a northwestern exhibit was given up because the parties promoting the enterprise failed to agree to meet the expenses necessary for a prolonged circuit of the northwestern cities. Both the Denver & Rio Grande and the Santa Fe Railway systems have extensively advertised the work of our members and I believe some appreciation of their efforts are due the officials who are responsible for this valuable assistance; that it should be expressed at this meeting.

Plans should also be made at the present time for a representative exhibit of our Society in the opening show to be held at an early date in the new museum building of the School of American Archeology in Santa Fe.[4]

There is a letter on hand requesting an exhibition in the auspices of the Denver Art Association to be held in September of this year. Many letters have been written by the secretary answering requests for information, in regard to exhibitions and the specific matters taken up by the Society at the last annual meeting.

The growing reputation of the Society and the increasing demands for its usefulness at home and abroad should encourage us to realize that no effort is wasted which we can employ for its advancement. I would like to say right here in connection with this that I feel that we are not all pulling together as well as we should; that there seems to be an apathy among the members and a feeling that the secretary must supply the initiative.

Bert G. Phillips
Secretary

Secretary & Treasurer's Report 1917

[Although dated 1917 by Bert Phillips, the reference to the war suggests he wrote this report in the summer of 1918.]

Looking back over the three years since the Taos Society of Artists was organized we are greatly encouraged by the success already achieved in spite of the fact that a great world war has raged during that time and that our own country has been taking part in it for over a year.

Our two circuit exhibitions now united at Colorado Springs have visited the cities of New York, Boston, Chicago, St. Louis, Des Moines, Denver, Santa Fe, Los Angeles, Pasadena, & Salt Lake City.

Our pictures have met with no little appreciation from thousands of people and a great deal of advertising matter has been printed and circulated until it would be difficult to find a person in the whole country making any pretention to being posted in art matters who has not heard of Taos and the "Taos Artists."

Several sales have been made in the exhibitions and we feel that had the world been at peace the number would have been more than doubled, so we look forward to the time when a very substantial reward will be the outcome of our efforts to keep the name of the organization before the public. In the year before us our efforts may be attended with greater difficulties but that is all the more reason why we should put forth our best endeavors.

The financial affairs of the Society have been handled in such a way that no great expenditure has been called for. Except for one printing bill amounting to $2.25 [?] the items of expense have mostly been for postage and telegrams. The balance brought forward was $3.80, collected for dues $9.00, making total of $12.80. Expended $6.80, leaving balance on hand of $6.00.

Bert G. Phillips, Sect. & Treas.

Minutes of the Third Annual Meeting of T.S.A. 1917

The third annual meeting of T.S.A. was held at the home of Mr. E. I. Couse July 15th 1917. On motion of the president minutes of the previous meeting were read and approved.

On motion by Mr. Blumenschein which was seconded and carried the By-Laws were changed to allow the election of members by majority vote of those present at the annual meeting instead of the unanimous vote.

Motion by Mr. Blumenschein that the secretary continue correspondence with the Denver Art Ass. relative to locating an exhibit of the T.S.A. Seconded & carried. Mr. Ufer & Mr. Higgins were elected as active members.

Motion by Mr. Blumenschein that an amendment be made to the Constitution, permitting members to exhibit only paintings of southwestern subjects in the circuit exhibitions of the T.S.A. Seconded & carried.

Motion by Mr. Higgins that a class of associate members be created having the right to exhibit with the Society and exempt from all dues. Seconded by Mr. Blumenschein & carried. Mr. Rolshoven was elected as an associate member.

A motion was made and carried requesting the secretary

to write letters of appreciation to Mr. Paul Walter, secretary of School of Amer. Research, Mr. W. H. Simpson of A.T. & Santa Fe Ry., Mr. F. A. Wadleigh of the D. & R.G. Ry., Mr. Gerson Gusdorf, Mrs. Pooler, of Taos, N.M.[5]

Meeting adjourned on motion by Mr. Berninghaus, seconded by Mr. Higgins.

[Special Meeting, August 13, 1917]

Special meeting was held at the home of Mr. Rolshoven Aug. 13th 1917 for the purpose of arranging two circuit exhibitions.

[Bert Phillips' notes reveal a proposed exhibition schedule as follows:]

Hotel Majestic, N.Y. Nov. 20 to Dec. 20.
R.C. & N.M. Vose, 394 & 398 Boylesten St.
Boston, Mass. Dec. 31 to Jan. 19.
Chicago Jan. 25 to Feb. 25. Ask commission. Must be in St. Louis to open March 1st.
Noonan-Kocian. St. Louis. Month of March.
Des Moines, Iowa for month of April.
Kansas City. Colorado Sprs.
Santa Fe. Pictures sold must be replaced.

[Special Meeting, September 16, 1917]

Special meeting was held at the home of Mr. Couse Sept. 16th 1917 to meet Mr. Paul Walter to discuss ways & means for starting western circuit in Santa Fe.

[Special Meeting (no date)]

Special meeting at Mr. Berninghaus' rooms. Motion by Mr. Blumenschein that associate members be required to pay annual dues was seconded by Mr. Ufer and carried.

1918

Minutes Fourth Annual Meeting
Taos Society of Artists

The fourth annual meeting of the Taos Society of Artists was held in the studio of Mr. E. I. Couse, July 16, 1918, with all members present. Minutes of the third annual meeting were read and approved.

Mr. Couse submitted a letter from Minneapolis, which asked for a collection of about thirty pictures, to be shown in that and other northern cities. It was agreed to comply with the request, and arrangements made with Mr. Couse in charge. The collection was made up from our exhibition then at Hardy's Gallery, in Colorado Springs.

Mr. Julius Rolshoven, who has been an associate member, was elected to active membership. Mr. Robert Henri, of New York, was elected an associate member.

Election of officers to serve for the ensuing year was then in order, and after some hesitancy on the part of the present president, Mr. Couse, he was again unanimously elected president.

Mr. O. E. Berninghaus, was elected secretary and treasurer.

A suggestion by Mr. Rolshoven, indicating the feeling in Santa Fe, toward linking the name Santa Fe with that of Taos, so that the Society may be known as the Santa Fe-Taos Society of Artists, did not meet with approval of members, and its consideration therefore deferred.

On recommendation of Mr. Higgins, it was agreed to hold an exhibition in Santa Fe, beginning about August 4, 1918. The exhibition to consist mainly of small canvases.

The annual circuit exhibition was then discussed, and on recommendation of Mr. Blumenschein, it was agreed to begin the circuit in January, 1919, in the galleries of E. C. Babcock,

New York, with Detroit, Chicago, and St. Louis to follow, and other cities to be arranged by our secretary.

Meeting adjourned on the motion of Mr. Phillips.

An adjourned meeting was called the following day, July 17, at which was discussed at length, the nomination of Mr. Burt Harwood, by Mr. Phillips, with a result that no action was to be taken at this time. However, at the suggestion of Mr. Rolshoven, it was agreed, owing to peculiar circumstances, that a letter be drafted and forwarded to Mr. Harwood, explaining the action and attitude of the Society.[6]

O. E. Berninghaus Sec. 7/11-19

Special Meeting August 26, 1918

After disposing of a few minor items, a proposal by Mr. Berninghaus to form a honorary membership class was on his motion, and seconded by Mr. Rolshoven, approved by all members.

On motion by Mr. Blumenschein, seconded by Mr. Higgins, Mr. Edgar L. Hewett, President of the Santa Fe Archeological Society, was unanimously elected an honorary member.[7]

On motion of Mr. Higgins, seconded by Mr. Phillips, Mr. Frank Springer, paleontologist, of Las Vegas, New Mexico, was unanimously elected an honorary member.[8]

Complying with a feeling among the members, that the Society's governing rules are somewhat indefinite, President Couse, submitted a resolution by which the Society may be governed by a Constitution and By-Laws, with a proposal to have same take effect at next annual meeting. The resolution was approved on motion by Ufer, and seconded by Mr. Rolshoven.

The president had appointed out of meeting, Mr. Higgins,

Berninghaus, and Couse, a committee to draft such Constitution and By-Laws, which was presented at this meeting. After lengthy discussion and consideration, and with a number of alterations, the Constitution and By-Laws herewith attached [were] finally adopted on motion of Mr. Ufer, and seconded by Mr. Rolshoven.

On motion of Mr. Blumenschein, and seconded by Mr. Ufer, it was agreed that the new Constitution and By-Laws, take effect, beginning at this meeting.

Mr. Phillips was elected member of the Governing Board. The meeting adjourned on motion of Mr. Rolshoven.

[Berninghaus appended the following comments on various other matters to the minutes of the August 26 meeting.]

On September 20, the Governing Board issued a letter to the Film Committee in which it authorized only such expense as may be incurred for shipping films from city to city.

During July, August, and part of September, the collection will be shown in Colorado Springs, at Clifford Hardy's galleries.

The exhibition will be sent to Santa Fe to open there about the 12th of September.

We have had requests for exhibitions from cities along the coast, namely, Seattle, Washington, and Los Angeles, California, but since we have not planned to arrange our circuit that far west, the request could not be accommodated at this time.

The press at all exhibition points have given us liberal and frequent space in their columns, commenting on the exhibition, and if this were compared with paid advertising, the space given us would amount to some $2500.00.

There were 110 letters received by the secretary, who in

turn has written 117 letters, and 110 special letters to individuals, calling their attention to the exhibition.

The report is respectfully submitted
O. E. Berninghaus Sec.

Special Meeting September 27, 1918,
With Mr. Herbert Dunton, Acting Secretary

All members present, excepting Phillips and Berninghaus.

The meeting was called in order to protest against an article which appeared in the September 14, issue of the *American Art News,* written by E. L. Blumenschein, which reflected most unpleasantly on the patriotism and attitude of our members, towards their activity in war work.[9]

After some discussion, Mr. Blumenschein volunteered to write a letter of apology, which was approved, and to be forwarded to the *American Art News,* together with a letter drafted by Mr. Higgins, and signed by all members present, requesting its publication.

Mr. Blumenschein read a circular letter which he had sent to various art organizations, outlining the activity in the Range Finder work, and the results accruing therefrom.[10]

Mr. Rolshoven, seconded by Blumenschein, recommended that all letters for publication, should first have the approval of the Governing Board. The motion was approved.

President Couse, requested Mr. Blumenschein to try and get a written word from Mr. Robert Ervien, relieving the Taos Society of Artists, from any loss or damage to the motion picture reels.[11] (A letter from Mr. Ervien, relieving the Society from responsibility was already in the hands of the secretary, who was not present to make mention of it).

The meeting adjourned on motion of Mr. Higgins.

O. E. Berninghaus
Sec. 7/11-19

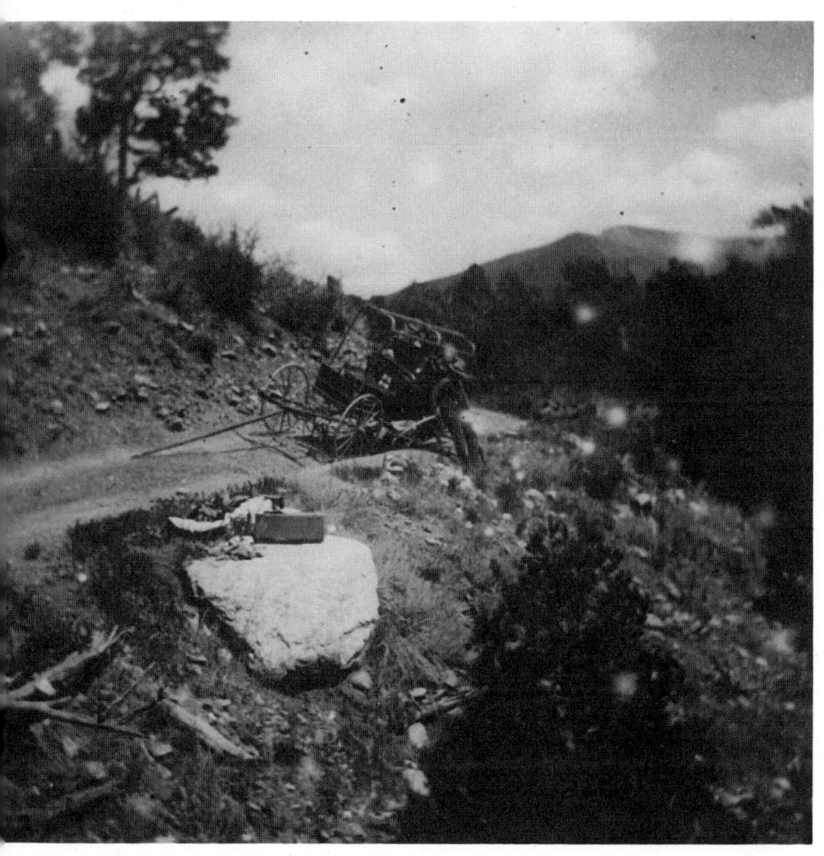

The broken wheel that first brought Ernest Blumenschein and Bert Phillips to Taos. Photo taken a few miles north of Taos on September 3, 1898. Courtesy Museum of New Mexico (neg. no. 40378). Photo by Bert Phillips.

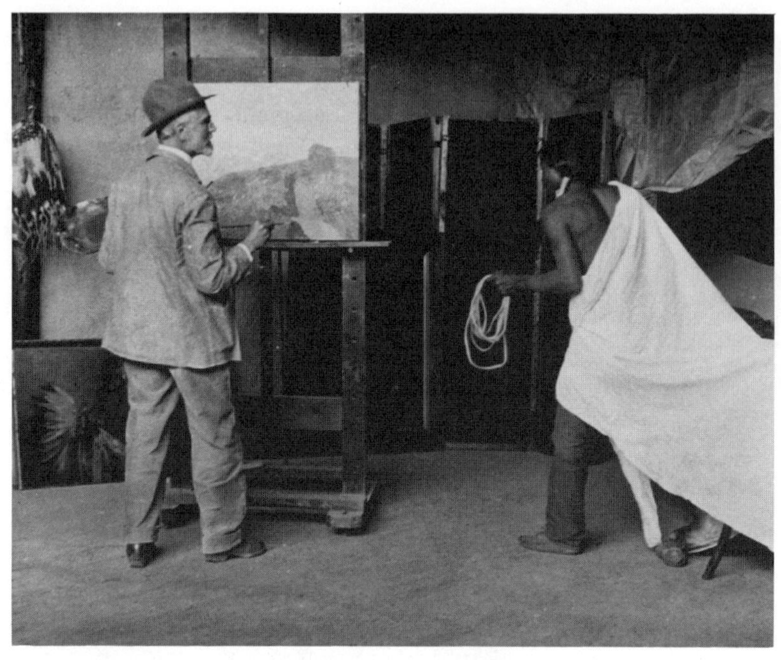

Joseph Henry Sharp, c. 1914–16. Courtesy Museum of New Mexico, Dunton Collection (neg. no. 116767).

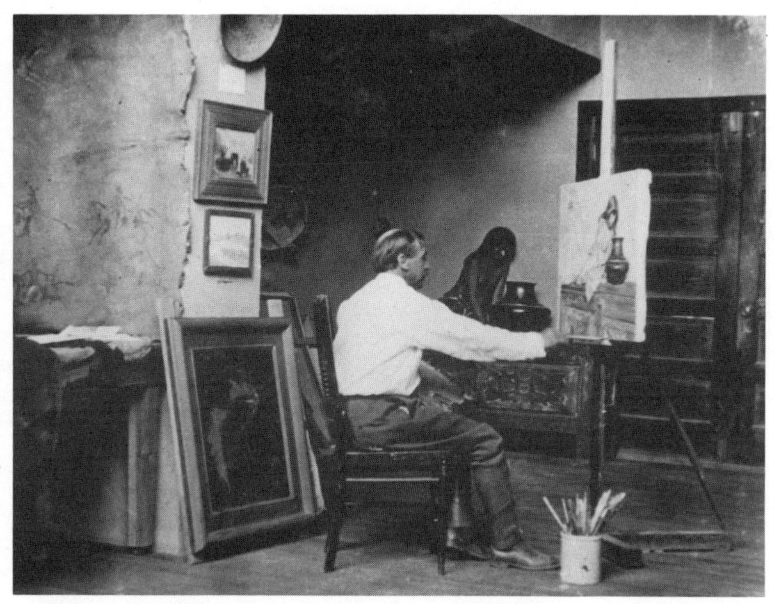

Bert Geer Phillips, c. 1914–16. The painting is entitled "The Secret Olla," and is now in the Santa Fe Collection of Southwestern Art. Courtesy Museum of New Mexico, Dunton Collection (neg. no. 116768).

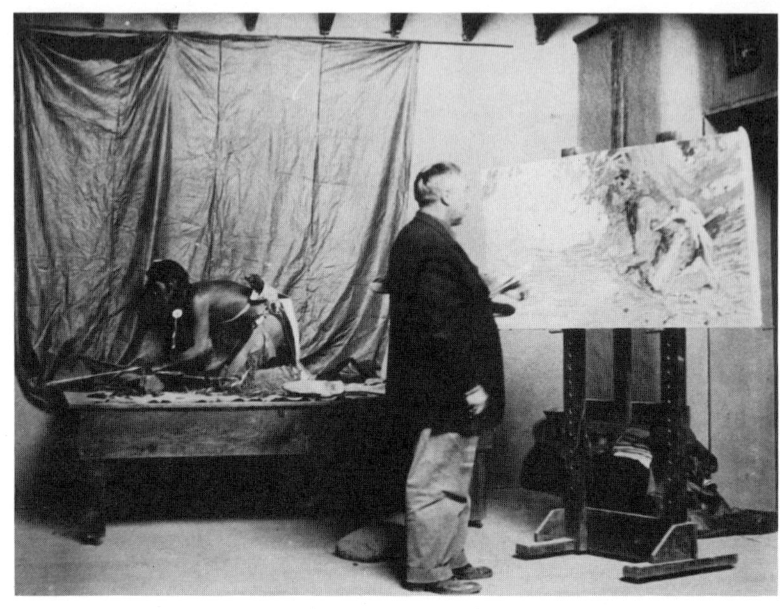

E. Irving Couse, c. 1914–16. Courtesy Museum of New Mexico, Dunton Collection (neg. no. 116771).

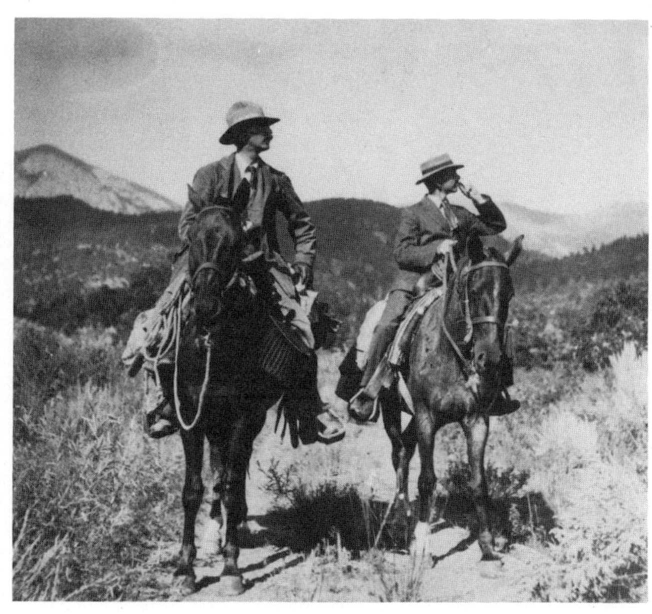

W. Herbert Dunton and Oscar E. Berninghaus on a hunting trip, c. 1914–16. Courtesy Museum of New Mexico, Dunton Collection (neg. no. 116649).

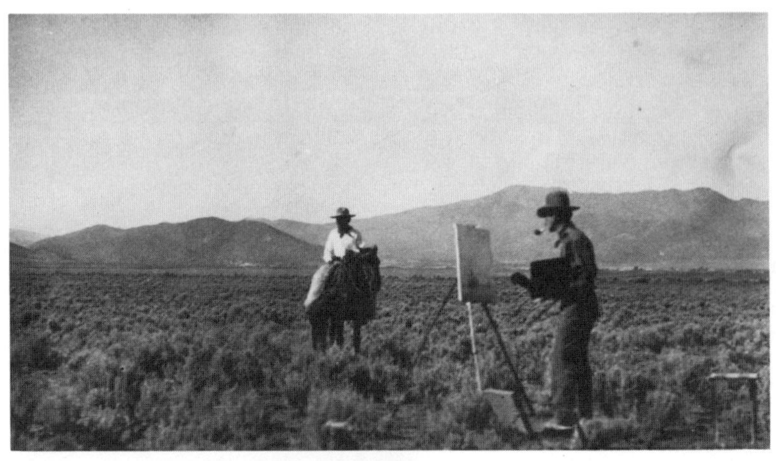

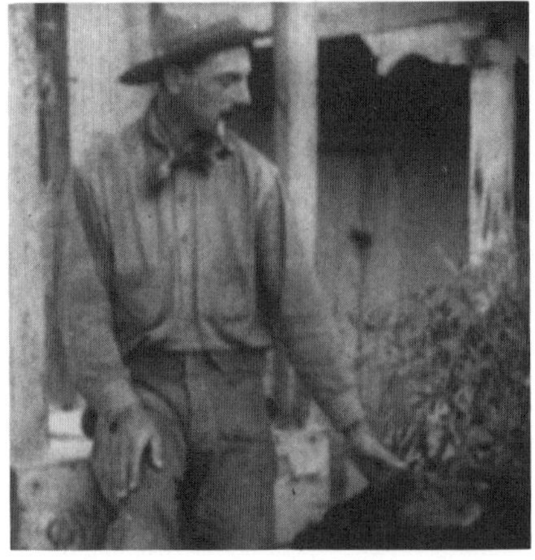

W. Herbert Dunton painting near Taos, c. 1914–16. Courtesy Museum of New Mexico, Dunton Collection (neg. no. 116772).

W. Herbert Dunton petting his dog at his home in Taos (now the Blumenschein home). This is a still from the 1917 motion picture "Adventures in Kit Carson Land." Courtesy State Records Center and Archives, Santa Fe.

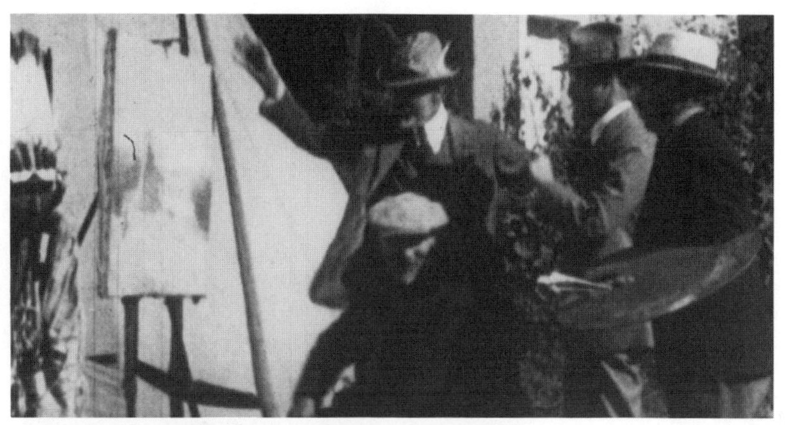

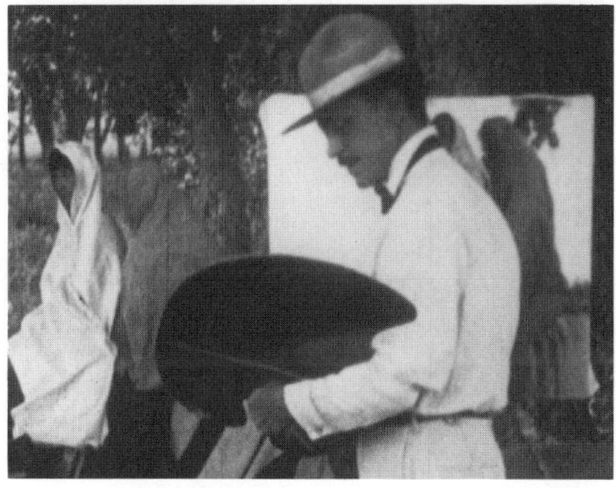

Irving Couse (seated) and (from left) Joseph Sharp, Ernest Blumenschein, and Bert Phillips, as shown in the 1917 motion picture "Adventures in Kit Carson Land." In this sequence, Phillips is painting, whereupon the other three artists walk up and begin joking with him. Courtesy State Records Center and Archives, Santa Fe.

Victor Higgins in Taos. This is a still from the 1917 motion picture "Adventures in Kit Carson Land." Courtesy State Records Center and Archives, Santa Fe.

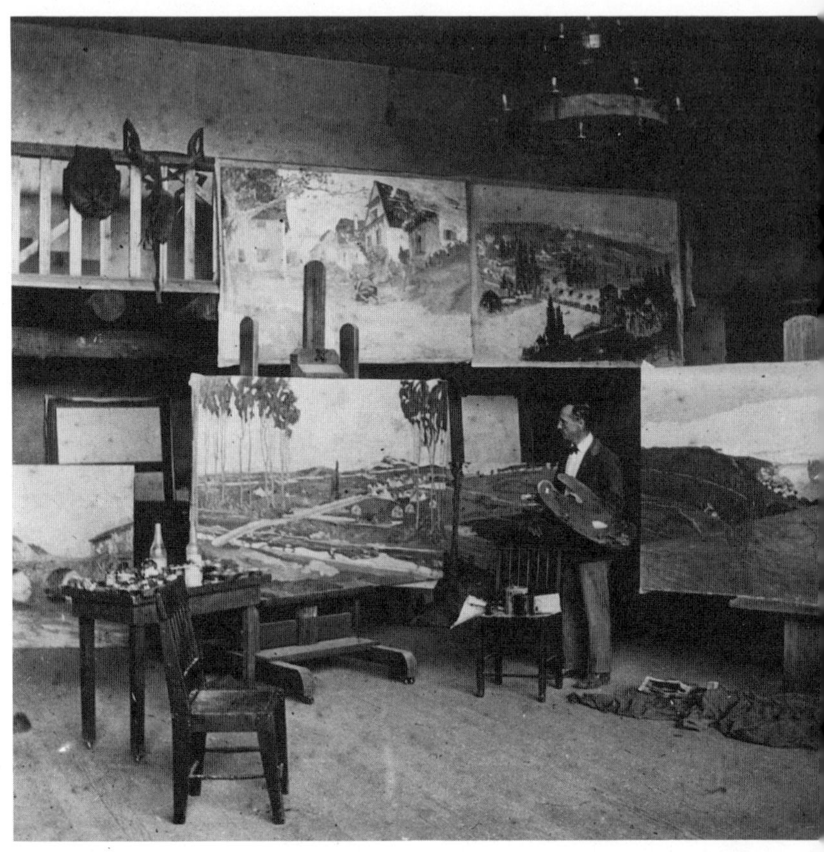

Ernest L. Blumenschein with a collection of "range-finder" paintings in 1918. These paintings of northern France and Belgium were sent to army training camps where they were used to instruct soldiers in estimating distances, detecting cover, and making maps. The painting at far left on the floor is by Harriett Blackstone; at center on the easel, by Walter Ufer; half hidden on the floor in front of Blumenschein, by W. Herbert Dunton; on the easel at far right, by Blumenschein. Hanging from the balcony railing, at the center, is a painting by Oscar Berninghaus, and to the right of it is a painting by Gustave Baumann. Courtesy Museum of New Mexico (neg. no. 15604).

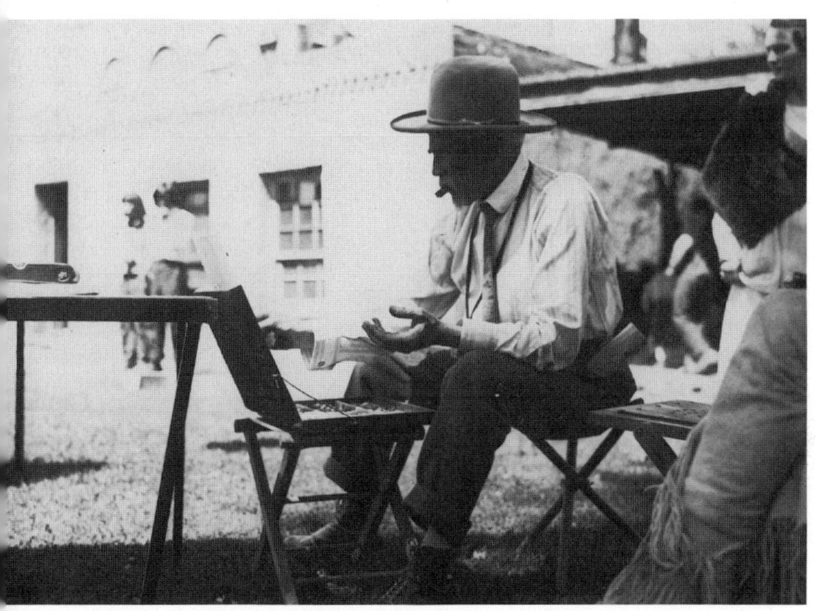

Julius Rolshoven sketching his model Santiago in the patio of the Palace of the Governors, Santa Fe, during the 1919 Fiesta. Courtesy Museum of New Mexico (neg. no. 10755). Photo by Wesley Bradfield.

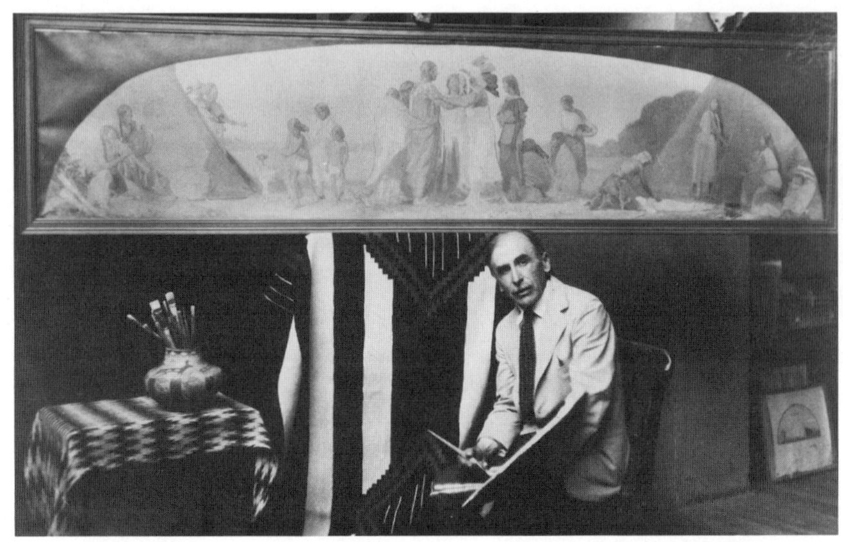

Bert G. Phillips. Courtesy Museum of New Mexico (neg. no. 19389).

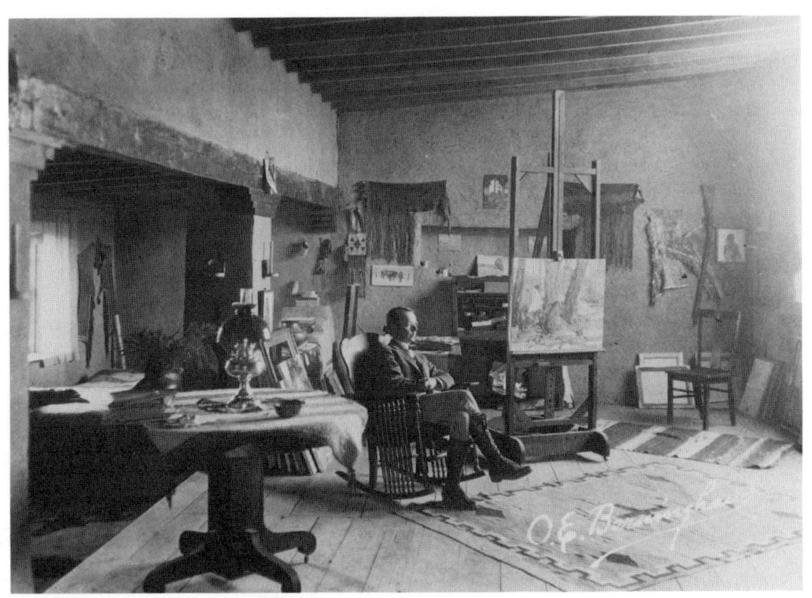

Oscar E. Berninghaus at his home in Taos. Courtesy Museum of New Mexico (neg. no. 40393).

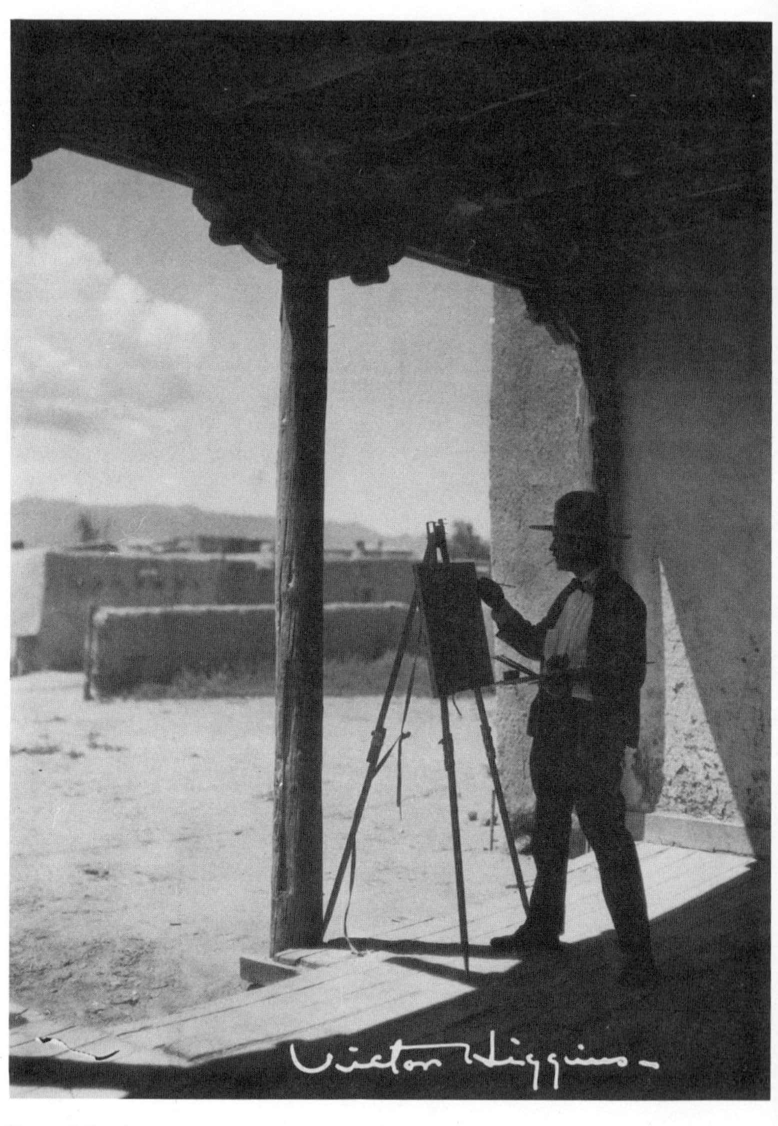

Victor Higgins. Courtesy Museum of New Mexico (neg. no. 40394).

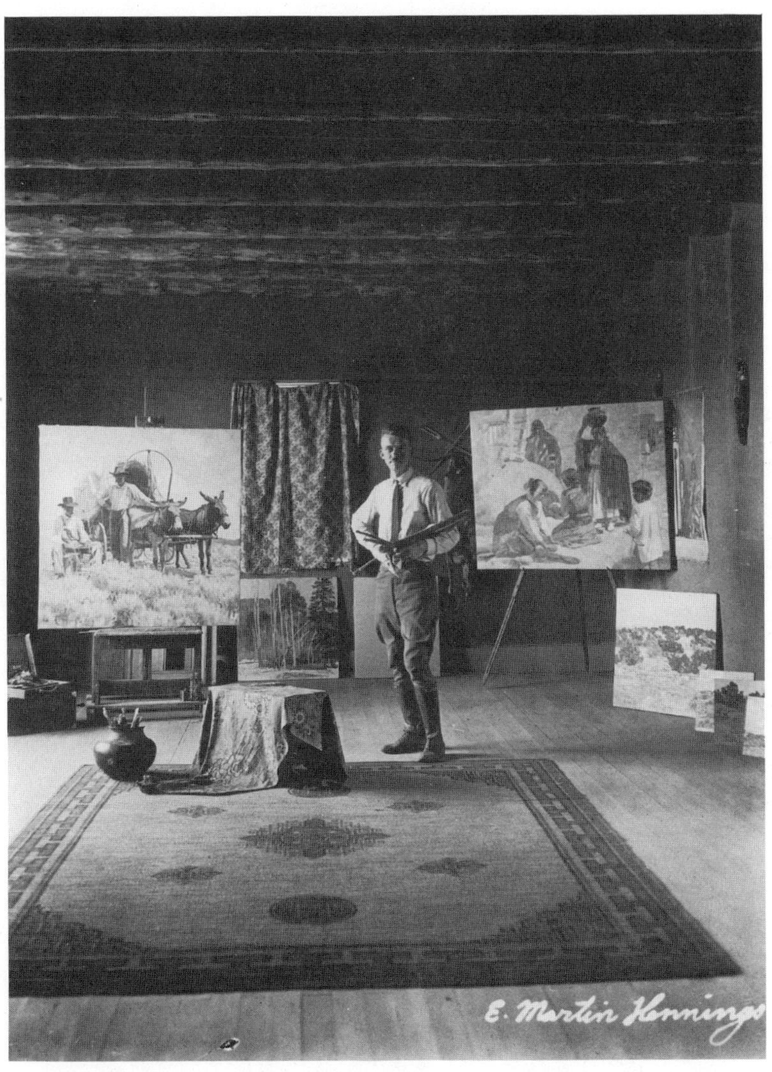

E. Martin Hennings in his studio in Taos, c. 1924. Courtesy Museum of New Mexico (neg. no. 40395).

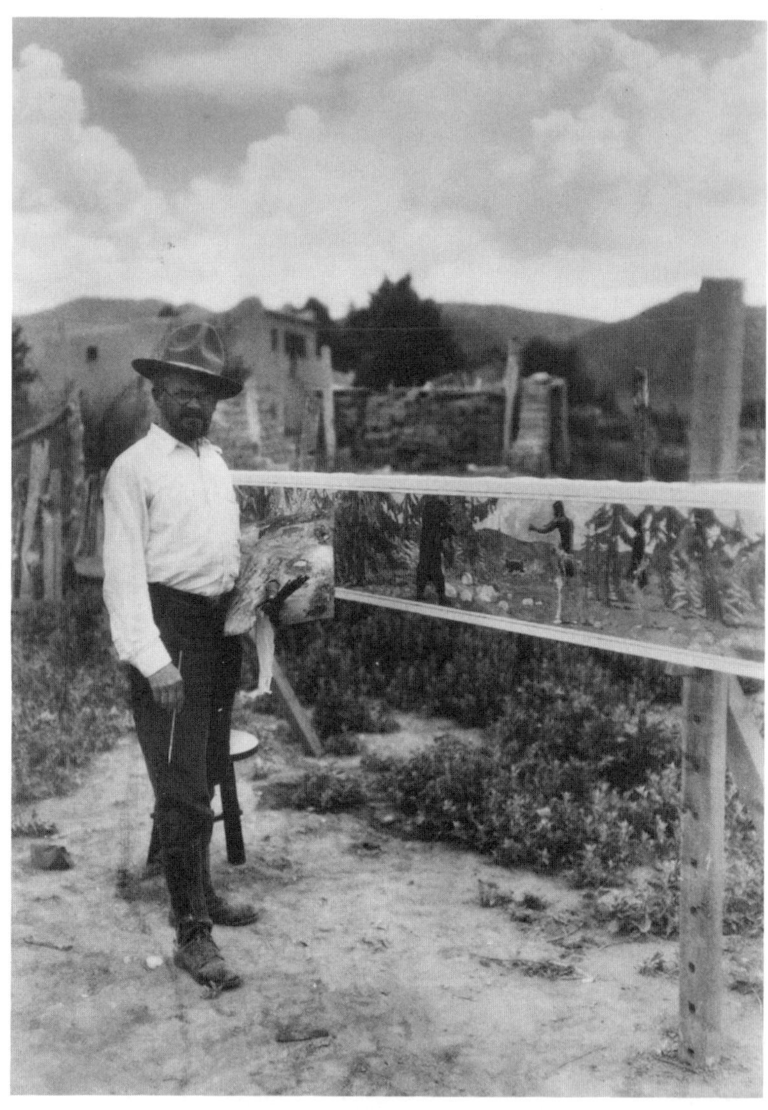

Walter Ufer in Taos. This was part of a mural 15 inches high by 70 feet long that was commissioned for a Wichita, Kansas, home (reference the *Taos Valley News,* December 27, 1924). Courtesy The Albuquerque Museum Photoarchives.

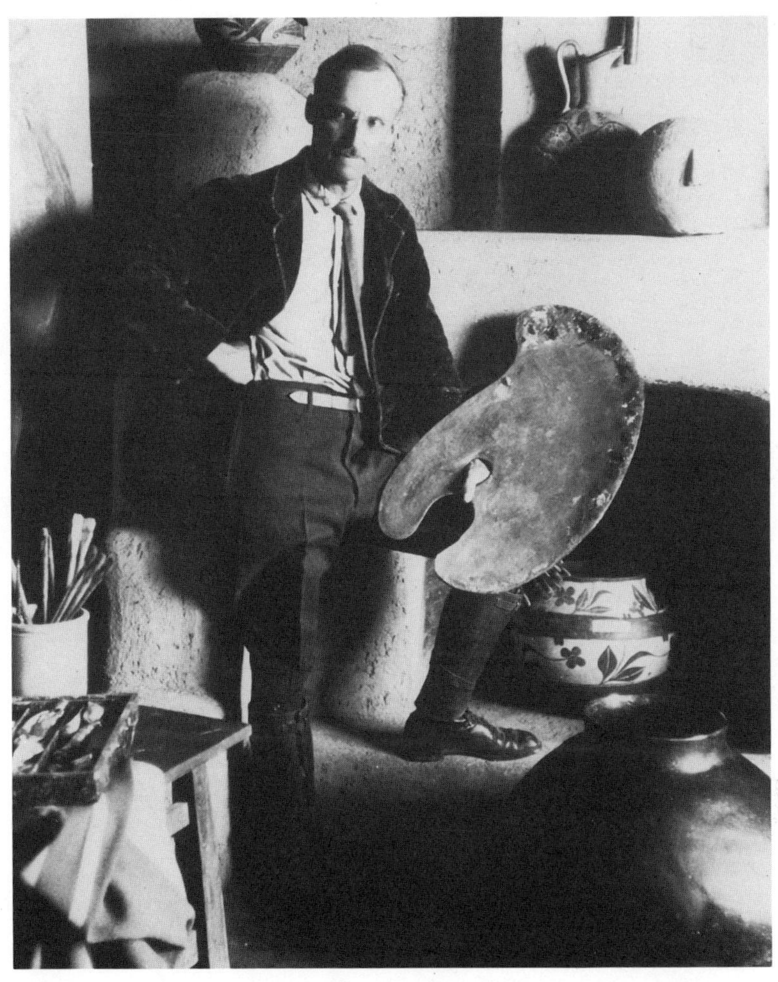

Ernest L. Blumenschein. Courtesy Museum of New Mexico (neg. no. 20566).

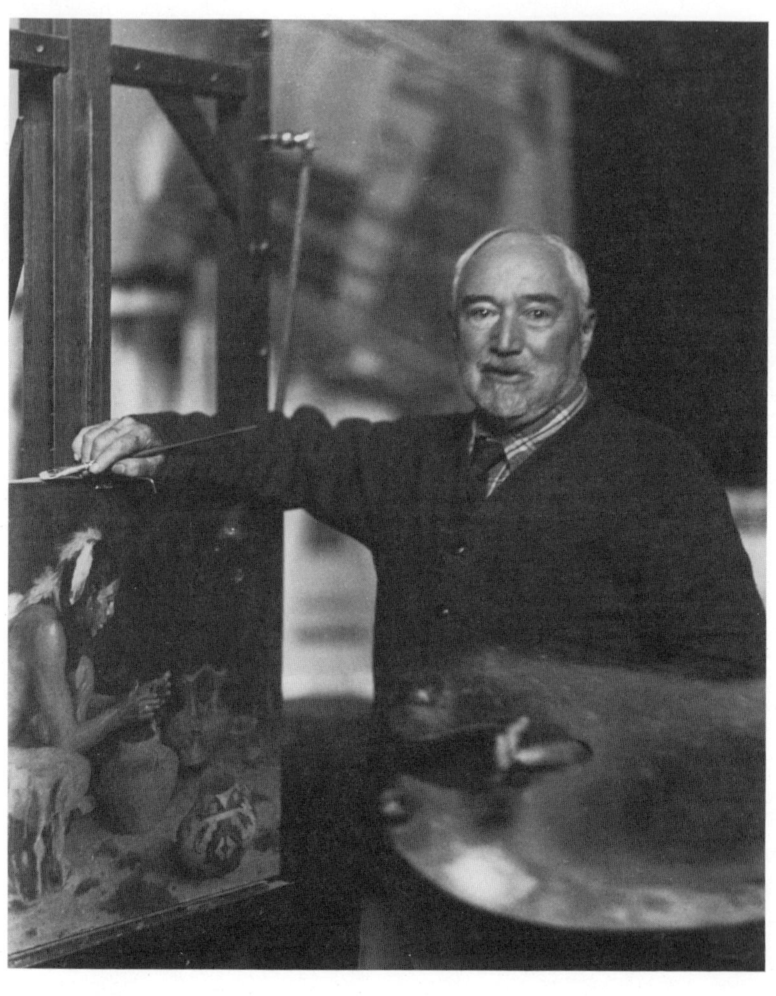

E. Irving Couse, 1932. Courtesy Museum of New Mexico (neg. no. 59753). Photo by Will Connell.

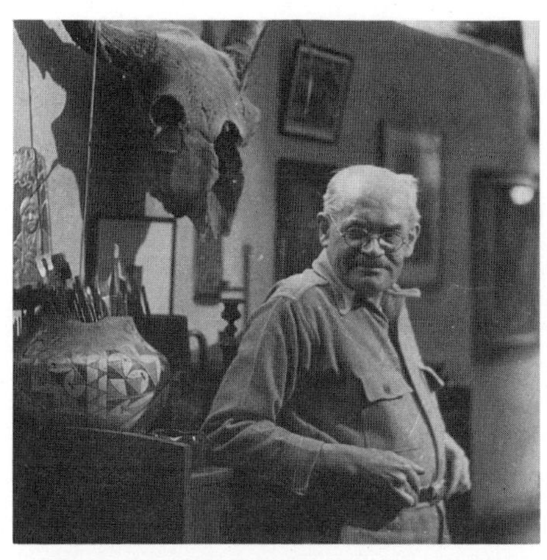

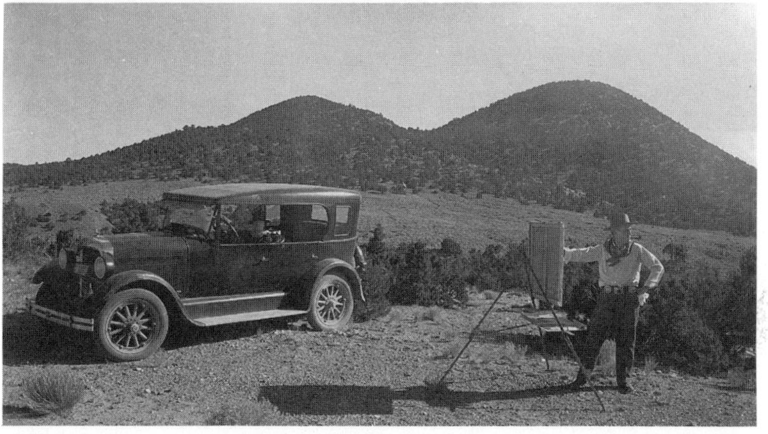

Walter Ufer, 1932. Courtesy Museum of New Mexico (neg. no. 42910). Photo by Will Connell.

John and Dolly Sloan near Santa Fe, 1926. Sloan was elected an associate member of the Taos Society of Artists in 1921. Courtesy Museum of New Mexico (neg. no. 28836). Photo by T. Harmon Parkhurst.

Minutes of the Taos Society of Artists

The first meeting took place at the home of Dr. Martin July 1915. Mr. Berninghaus was elected temporary chairman. Mr. E. I. Couse was elected President and B. G. Phillips was elected Treasurer & Secretary. The members present were Mr. E. I. Couse, Mr. J. H. Sharp, Mr. O. E. Berninghaus, Mr. W. H. Dunton & Mr. B. G. Phillips. Mr. E. L. Blumenschein was absent. The name of the organization was discussed and 'Taos Society of Artists' was selected. By unanimous vote it was decided that new ~~members must be proposed~~ applicants for membership in the society must be proposed

The first page of the minutes of the first annual meeting of the Taos Society of Artists, July 1915. Courtesy Museum of New Mexico.

The Taos Society of Artists

Ernest L. Blumenschein, A. N. A.
President
Taos, New Mexico
Walter Ufer, A. N. A.
Secretary and Treasurer
Taos, New Mexico

8th Annual Meeting
Minutes –

Annual Meeting July 12th 1922
T. S. of A.

The meeting was called to order by the President Mr. E. L. Blumenschein at 8 25 P.M., members present were Berninghaus Blumenschein, Couse, Phillips, Sharp & Ufer.

The report of the annual meeting of July 12th 1921 was read, approved & carried.

The report of the Secretary and Treasurer was read approved & carried.

Letters about the 1922 circuit showing were the exhibit is located, and where it will proceed to assure members were read. Letter of American Fed. of Arts asking for a group exhibition was read. It was by vote decided to write the Federation that invidual members would exhibit if they were asked, but that at the present time could be sent at present, but would be considered in the future.

Report from Herbert Dunton as Chairman of the Entertainment committee was read approved & carried.

Thereupon Mr. Dunton's Resignation was read, and it was decided

The first page of the minutes of the 1922 annual meeting, Taos Society of Artists. Courtesy Museum of New Mexico.

1924

Minutes of Annual Meeting of the Taos Society of Artists July 12th 1924

The Taos Society of Artists

The 10th annual meeting of the T.S.A. was held at the studio of E Irving Couse on July 12th 1924. The meeting was called to order at 8.30 P.M. E. I. Couse the officer of the Society occupying the chair. Members present O. E. Berninghaus. E. I. Couse. B. G. Phillips J H Sharp & Walter Ufer.

The minutes of the last meeting held July 31 '23 were read & approved

Report of the officer regarding circuit exhibitions & matters of general interest read & approved. Financial report showing a balance of funds in the treasury of $51.20 read & approved.

Election of new members.—

Miss Catherine Critcher & Mr E. Martin Hennings were unanimously elected to active membership. The name of W. Herbert Dunton was withdrawn from nomination after a lengthy discussion during which it developed that it was the sense of the ~~members~~ meeting that Mr Duntons previous resignation from the Society was due to the fact that he had refused to consider an election as secretary & an election to membership at the present time would be inadvisable untill he would agree to fulfill what was considered a former obligation.

Owing to the absence of Victor Higgins the new official for the coming year ~~the~~ no new business was discussed & the meeting adjourned at 10 o'clock

E. Irving Couse.

Minutes of the 1924 annual meeting, Taos Society of Artists. Courtesy Museum of New Mexico.

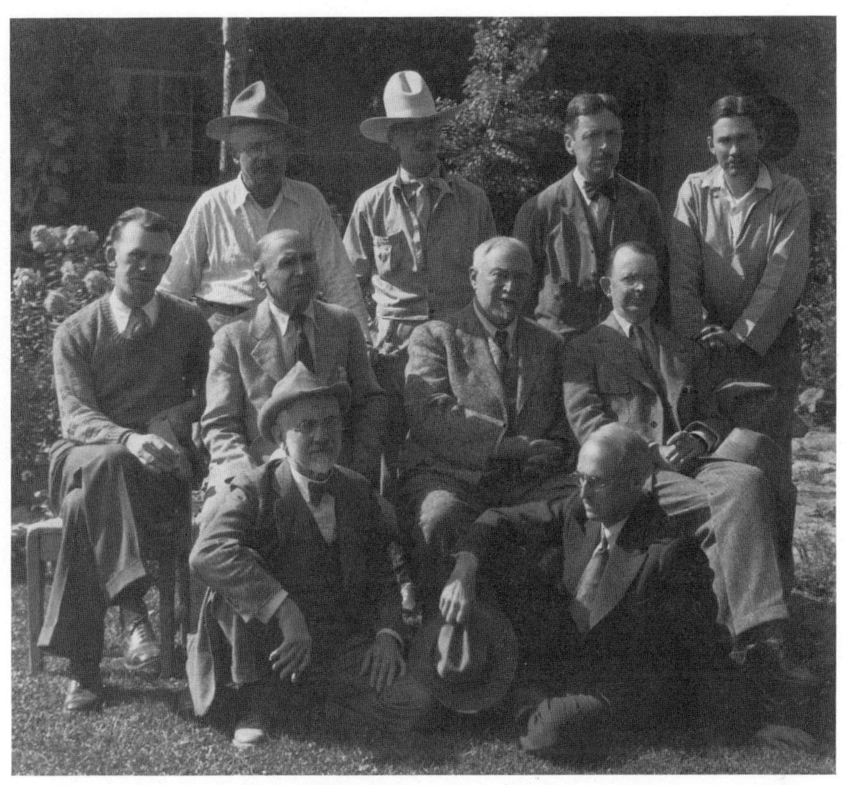

Ten former members of the Taos Society of Artists in the garden of E. I. Couse in Taos in the summer of 1932. Standing left to right: Walter Ufer, W. Herbert Dunton, Victor Higgins, Kenneth M. Adams. Seated left to right: E. Martin Hennings, Bert G. Phillips, E. Irving Couse, Oscar E. Berninghaus. Front row left to right: Joseph H. Sharp, Ernest L. Blumenschein. Courtesy Museum of New Mexico (neg. no. 28817). Photo by C. E. Lord.

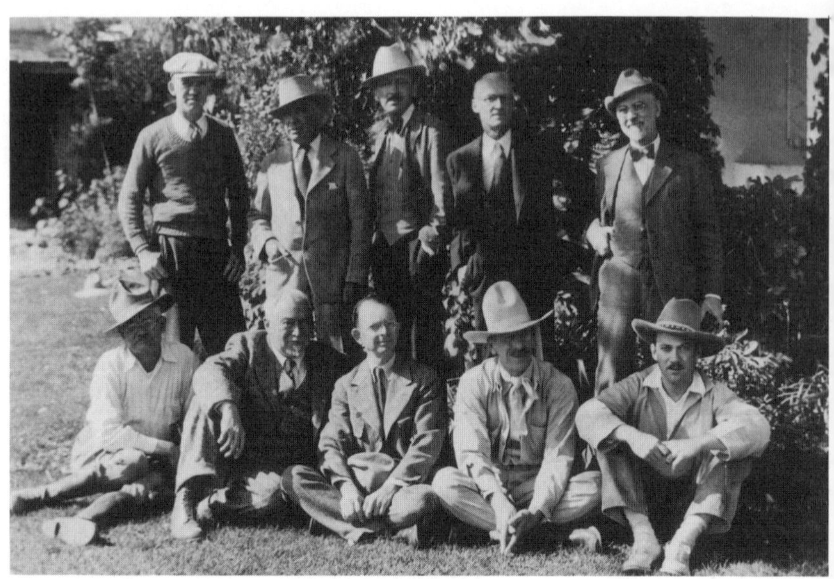

A second photograph of ten former members of the Taos Society of Artists in the garden of E. I. Couse in Taos in the summer of 1932. Standing left to right: E. Martin Hennings, Bert G. Phillips, Victor Higgins, Ernest L. Blumenschein, Joseph H. Sharp. Seated left to right: Walter Ufer, E. Irving Couse, Oscar E. Berninghaus, W. Herbert Dunton, and Kenneth M. Adams. Courtesy Kit Carson Historic Museums, Taos. Photo by C. E. Lord.

1919

Report of Secretary
Taos Society of Artists
For Season 1918–1919

At the last meeting of the Society, July 16, 1918, Mr. Julius Rolshoven was made an active member, and Mr. Robert Henri, of New York, who is more closely identified with the Santa Fe Art Colony, was elected an associate member, and upon being so notified, responded in a gracious letter of acceptance.

Membership to date—9 active and 1 associate.

Several special meetings of the Society were held after the annual meeting, as follows:

Meeting August 8, 1918, at Mr. Berninghaus' studio.

At this meeting was discussed a letter from Mr. E. C. Babcock, of New York, where exhibition circuit was to begin, relative to express charges which he declined to pay on receiving and forwarding the collection of paintings, constituting the exhibition. It was agreed by all members present that members send their paintings prepaid, and that arrangements be made to have following exhibition point pay express from New York, thus relieving Mr. Babcock of any express expense.

In appreciation of the gift of an album of photographs, and the loan of a set of moving picture reels, showing the artists of Taos, by Mr. Robert Ervien, of Santa Fe, it was recommended by Mr. Blumenschein and approved, that some form of recognition be extended to Mr. Ervien, and it was agreed that a portfolio containing a sketch from each member be appropriate, and presented to him. Mr. Couse appointed Mr. Ufer a committee of one to collect and arrange the sketches in some suitable form (the portfolio was sent to Mr. Ervien on August 28, who acknowledged receipt with many thanks).

Moving Picture Reels

In order to properly place the moving picture reels to be shown in cities, where our exhibition is to be held, Mr. Couse appointed Mr. Blumenschein chairman of a committee, with Mr. Rolshoven, Higgins, and Berninghaus, to assist in making the proper arrangements.

Exhibitions of 1919

Our exhibition circuit began in New York City, opening there in the galleries of E. C. Babcock. All members were represented in the exhibition, excepting Mr. Higgins and Ufer, the latter's pictures having failed to arrive during the period of exhibition. Three canvases were sold here, namely, one each of Henri, Dunton, and Blumenschein. Mr. Couse, who had charge of the exhibition at this point can perhaps tell how well the public was interested.

The exhibition was next shown at the Detroit Museum of Art in February, with all members represented. The authorities here were very courteous in their activities and welcome toward the exhibition, but their impressions of the merit of the collection was not encouraging, as evidenced by their letter summarizing the collection at the close of the exhibition. No sales.

Chicago was the next exhibition point, showing there at Carson Pirie Scott & Company, during the month of March. A good deal of attention was given the show, both by the public and artists. The impression prevailed that the collection was not as strong as last year's exhibition. No sales.

St. Louis was the next point, showing there in April, at Noonan-Kocian Galleries. The St. Louis Art League held a reception and tea in honor of the Society and its members, on the afternoon of April 14, which was well attended. The motion pictures of the artists were shown in an adjoining gallery, and created considerable interest, and required showing them four times to comply with the wishes of late-comers. Three pictures were sold here, namely, two by Mr. Ufer, and one by Berninghaus. Seventy-five personal letters were written by the secretary to St. Louis acquaintances, calling special attention to the work of the members, whose work they may not be familiar with.

The exhibition next went to Kansas City, showing there during the month of May, at Hug & Sarachek Galleries. Kansas City being a new field for the exhibition, a considerable amount of work was necessary to interest the people of that city—and accordingly a number of personal letters were written to officers and directors of various organizations such as the Chamber of Commerce, City Club, Atheneum Club, and a number of people. Also, the press calling attention to the exhibition and [giving] their cooperation. 3 pictures were sold here—two by E. I. Couse and one by Ufer. Hug & Sarachek request that the exhibition be again shown at their gallery next season.

Minutes of the Fifth Annual Meeting
Taos Society of Artists

The fifth annual meeting of the Taos Society of Artists was held in the studio of O. E. Berninghaus, July 11th, 1919, members present Couse, Phillips, Blumenschein, Dunton, Ufer, Sharp and Berninghaus. Members Rolshoven and Henri were not in town.

President Couse read an interesting report of his activities and of the exhibition which visited Minneapolis, St. Paul, Grand Rapids and other cities. He stated that inasmuch as the exhibitions of the Society have become an event of the year in many cities, he desired to impress the members of the importance of sending their very best works to all our exhibitions. In closing he stated that he had been president of the Society for three successive years and desired that someone other than he should be chosen for the ensuing year.

The report of the secretary & treasurer was read and approved.

The treasurer's report showing a balance of $25.83 was read and approved.

A report of the exhibition circuit was read and showed that the exhibition visited New York, Detroit, Chicago, St. Louis, Kansas City and was next to be shown in Colorado Springs and later at Santa Fe, New Mexico. Up to the time of this meeting ten pictures had been sold, namely, three in New York, three in St. Louis and four in Kansas City.

Mr. Blumenschein gave a report of the Film Committee and explained the difficulties he had encountered to display them. They were, however, shown in St. Louis to an interested and appreciative audience.

A resolution was presented by President Couse to change the By-Laws to read as follows:

The membership of the Society shall consist of American citizens and divided into the following classes: viz: Active, Associate and Honorary. After some discussion the resolution was adopted.

A letter from the Arizona State Fair, asking for our exhibition during the period of the Fair was read and after some discussion was thought not feasible. This also concerned a similar request from the Iowa State Fair at Des Moines, Iowa.

The continuance of our exhibition circuit after leaving Santa Fe was thought advisable and that the South with such places as El Paso, Fort Worth, New Orleans and other large places be visited and ultimately again to reach the eastern cities.

President Couse appointed Mr. Dunton to take charge of the exhibition after it leaves Santa Fe.

The Film Committee with Mr. Blumenschein as chairman, was reappointed and instructed to make effort to have the films shown at points where future exhibitions are to be held.

Mr. Ufer submitted for approval a proposition that each member contribute a painting to be donated to the new Battleship New Mexico. After a little discussion it was thought advisable to abandon the idea.

The new exhibition circuit for 1920 was then discussed and it was recommended that the exhibition begin in New York in the galleries of E. & I. Milch, with Philadelphia, Cincinnati, Chicago, St. Louis, Kansas City and Colorado Springs to follow.

The nomination of Mr. Albert Groll, New York, for associate membership, was approved on motion by Ufer and seconded by Phillips. The secretary was instructed to notify Mr. Groll of his election.

An expense item of $5.00 for projecting the films in St. Louis was allowed to Berninghaus.

The election of officers to serve for the ensuing year was then in order and the old officers reelected, namely, Mr. Couse, president, O. E. Berninghaus, secretary & treasurer and Bert Phillips, a member of the Board.

O. E. Berninghaus
Sec. 1920

1920

Report of the Secretary
Taos Society of Artists
1919 and 1920

The Society's membership at present consists of nine active and two associate members, whose names are as follows:

Active: O. E. Berninghaus, E. L. Blumenschein, E. I. Couse, W. Herbert Dunton, Victor Higgins, J. H. Sharp, Bert Phillips, Julius Rolshoven and Walter Ufer.

Associate: Robert Henri and Albert Groll.

At the last meeting of [the] Society, July 11th, 1919, Mr. Albert Groll of New York was elected an associate member of the Society and upon being so notified responded with a letter of acceptance.

One special meeting was called by the president for Oct. 30, 1919, for the purpose of taking action in the case of one Henry Balink, and it was unanimously voted by all members present that a letter be drafted requesting his deportation from this country.[12] Members present at this meeting: Couse, Blumenschein, Dunton, Higgins, Phillips and Ufer.

At this time last year our 1919 exhibition was in Kansas City, report of which was included in [the] secretary's report at that time. The collection was next shown at Colorado Springs during July, August, and part of September in the galleries of Clifford Hardy; two sales were made here.

The collection was next shown in Santa Fe during the month of October and part of November—no sales here.

As stated in the minutes of 1919, Mr. Dunton was appointed to take charge of the exhibition after its close at Santa Fe and to arrange a tour thru the southern states. Mr. Dunton later declined to act and accordingly after much discussion at an informal meeting on July 23rd, 1919, Mr. Ufer and Higgins volunteered for this service, to take charge after the exhibition at Albuquerque from which place we had in the meantime received and accepted an invitation to exhibit our collection from the Chamber of Commerce in that town.

The exhibition here was ill-fated and many unpleasant mix-ups occurred which resulted in the showing here being a failure. Thru some mismanagement on the part of the Albuquerque authorities the entire collection was returned to Santa Fe, they doing so without authority from us and solely on the belief that Santa Fe was the headquarters for our pictures, and in spite of the fact that they were repeatedly told to hold the collection for definite shipping instructions pending Mr. Ufer's success in arranging an exhibition point to follow. Ufer failing in this, instructions were immediately sent to forward the pictures to the individual artists. At this time the pictures had already been sent to Santa Fe and they in turn forwarded the pictures at the expense of the artists.

The secretary immediately communicated with Albuquerque about these express charges, asking for a refund, but with no satisfaction.

During this time complaints came in from the artists because of the very poor packing and the consequent dilapidated condition of their canvases when returned to them. Canvases and frames by Sharp, Ufer and Dunton were among those damaged and in Ufer's case as he states it, he doubts whether anything can be done with his picture. In accordance with his request and that of the president a claim for the amount of his damage was made known to Albuquerque together with a statement and another request for the refund of express charges. This brought no response of any kind and as far as the secretary can see it is hardly likely that anything can be done with this unfortunate affair.

Our 1920 exhibition circuit opened at Milch Galleries in

New York City on Jan. 17th and continued for two weeks. It was next shown in Cleveland, then at Cincinnati, St. Louis, Kansas City and is now in Colorado Springs. Shipping conditions were such that it was impossible to have the exhibition in these various places open on schedule time—it arrived in Kansas City almost a month after date arranged.

At all these points many letters were written by the secretary to various people, organizations, the press, etc., calling attention to our pictures and the work of the Society.

At St. Louis the moving picture films were again shown during the period of exhibition here. They were shown at the Columbia Theatre and one of the high class west-end movie theatres.

In contrast to the report of last year in which the sale of twelve canvases was reported, it is regrettable to report that no sales had thus far been made on the 1920 exhibition.

Several requests for our exhibitions have been made from several cities, namely, Denver and Nashville, Tenn. Owing to dates being already arranged, it was impossible to accommodate them—Nashville however is very anxious to have our collection and has set aside the month of November for us. They have however not indicated their willingness to agree to our terms. It may be well therefore for the next secretary to make note of this.

The secretary made an effort to have Des Moines, Iowa, show our collection during June in order to fill in between the Kansas City and Colorado Springs engagements, but we could not be accommodated. They however showed a keen desire to have our exhibition during some late fall or winter month—this may also be well for the next secretary to note.

The press has again given us liberal space in its columns in all cities where [the] exhibition was shown. There was, though, nothing new in these articles and the secretary feels that some steps should be taken towards creating a new interest thru some . . . publicity and recommends that a new story on different lines about the Society's work, its efforts, etc. be written. This should be sent to all newspapers thruout the country and should be sent in advance to cities where the exhibition is to be shown.

There were 129 letters, etc., received by the secretary who in turn has written 141 letters, etc., including 53 letters to individuals calling attention to the exhibition.

The report is respectfully submitted.

O. E. Berninghaus
Sec'y

Minutes of the Sixth Annual Meeting
Taos Society of Artists

The sixth annual meeting of the Taos Society of Artists was held at the studio of Mr. O. E. Berninghaus, July 12th 1920, at 8:30 P.M. Members Couse, Blumenschein, Phillips, Sharp, Higgins, Berninghaus and Ufer, were present. Mr. Dunton was in town, but excused himself as too busy to attend the meeting. Members Henri, Rolshoven, and Groll were not in town.

Mr. E. I. Couse, president, opened the meeting.

The reports of the secretary and treasurer (Berninghaus) were read, and approved. The treasurer's report showed a balance of $4.46 and was approved.

Mr. Blumenschein gave a report of the Films Committee, and explained the difficulties he had encountered to display them. A resolution was adopted to ask the State of New Mexico to present the Society with the films. Mr. Blumenschein was again appointed by Mr. Couse as the head of the Film Committee for the following year.

Mr. Ufer gave his report of the southern circuit, and which for the time being was dropped.

Thereupon the election of officers for the following year took place. It was motioned and seconded that the new officers should be elected by direct ballot, and that a majority should elect them. No nominees should be appointed.

Mr. E. I. Couse, president of the Society since its organization resigned his office, and Mr. O. E. Berninghaus, secretary and treasurer for the last three years, resigned his office.

On the first ballot taken Mr. E. L. Blumenschein proved a majority and was elected president.

On the first ballot taken Walter Ufer proved a majority, and was elected secretary and treasurer.

On the second ballot taken Mr. Victor Higgins proved a majority, and was elected to the Governing Board, now consisting of Blumenschein, Higgins and Ufer.

Following this the three new officers accepted their new positions, and thereupon Mr. Blumenschein took the chair as president, and continued the meeting. Walter Ufer took his place as secretary and treasurer, and continued the notation of minutes.

Mr. Victor Higgins motioned and seconded by Mr. Bert Phillips to give the ex-president Mr. E. I. Couse, a rising vote of thanks for his excellent and faithful services as president since the organization of the Society. This was loudly applauded and the entire Society present rose from their seats in honor of Mr. Couse.

This was followed by the members acting in the same way in honor of the excellent services given the Society, to Mr. O. E. Berninghaus, now ex-secretary and treasurer.

Thereupon Mr. Berninghaus treated the members of the Society present with refreshments.

At the time of this meeting our 1920 circuit was in Colorado Springs, and it was agreed upon to have this exhibition go to Des Moines, Iowa, if possible, the last two weeks in October, and to communicate with the Nashville Art Association at Nashville, Tennessee to take this circuit in November, and to ask them to pay for the return of the paintings to the various studios of the individual artists at their own expense if possible, and that this circuit should then be considered disbanded.

It was next agreed upon to start the 1921 circuit at the Milch Galleries of New York City if possible, and to follow this in Philadelphia, Cleveland, Cincinnati, Chicago, St. Louis, Kansas City, Colorado Springs, Des Moines, and Nashville if possible.

It was motioned, seconded and carried to not exhibit paintings over 36 inches in size, longest length for the 1921 circuit. Meeting adjourned.

Motioned, seconded and carried to approve with corrections. These corrections were made in the above minutes and therefore signed.

Signed,
Walter Ufer
Secretary & Treasurer.

Minutes of the Meeting held August 8th, 1920
of the Taos Society of Artists
at Blumenschein's Residence in Taos, 8:00 P.M.

Meeting was opened as promptly as possible by Mr. E. L. Blumenschein, president. Members present were Couse, Phillips, Sharp, Dunton, Berninghaus, Higgins, Blumenschein, and Ufer.

Mr. E. L. Blumenschein explained to the members why he called the meeting as it had to do with the 1921 circuit, and to agree upon a means possible by which the Society could be properly advertised in the newspapers, periodicals, museums and those desiring information about the Society.

Mr. Blumenschein thereupon appointed Mr. Dunton to write an article describing Taos and its surroundings. He appointed Mr. Higgins to write an article dealing with the artistic possibilities pertaining to Taos and surroundings and appointed Mr. Phillips to write an article dealing with the biographical.

These articles to be signed, and ready by August 29th, and if approved by the Society, to be printed in pamphlet form to be distributed where found necessary.

It was then followed by a discussion which took place in order to build and strengthen, if possible, our 1921 circuit.

It was motioned, seconded and carried to invite three artists from Santa Fe, New Mexico, namely: Sloan, Davey and Nordfeldt with one picture each to exhibit with us in our 1921 circuit.

A committee of three was named, Blumenschein, Higgins and Ufer, who on their way to Santo Domingo's Corn Dance should pay these artists a visit and sound them in their willingness to exhibit with us in our 1921 circuit.

A discussion took place as to whether the Society should erect a sign in the plaza of Taos or in the lobby of the Hotel of Taos, calling to the attention of the visitors to Taos that the artists who were members of the Taos Society of Artists do not solicit the sale of their paintings, that their aims toward others were proper and their professional etiquette of a high standing.

After drawing up the following wording for such a sign "the Taos Society of Artists does not approve of soliciting but would be glad to receive visitors and show their works upon request and after four P.M."

After much discussion it was decided to lay this matter for

awhile on the table. Refreshments were served and meeting adjourned.

Motion seconded and approved.	Signed, Walter Ufer Secretary & Treasurer.

Minutes of the Meeting held August 24th, 1920
of the Taos Society of Artists
at Blumenschein's Residence in Taos, 8:15 P.M.

The president opened the meeting at 8:15 P.M. Members Sharp, Higgins, Couse, Dunton, Berninghaus, Blumenschein and Ufer, were present. Members Henri, Rolshoven, Groll and Phillips were absent.

The reports and minutes of the secretary and treasurer of the last annual meeting, and of the meeting of the 8th, were read and approved with corrections which were made at the time of the meeting.

The president now gave his report of the Santa Fe trip, and visit to Mr. Sloan, Davey and Nordfeldt.

The secretary next read the business letters of the Society.

Mr. Dunton next read his written article, asking that nothing be changed in it without his consent. The article was called "The Painters—Taos," and [was] about one thousand words. The members present asking Dunton to sell this article to some magazine with photographs if possible so that we could print it in pamphlet form afterwards. Couse moved that Dunton's article be accepted with thanks which was carried.[13]

Mr. Higgins did not have his article written and his time was extended to September 20th.

It was moved to get the exhibition 1921 circuit on Fifth Avenue, New York City if possible and therefore to write to John Lavy for the lower gallery for the last two weeks in November or the first two in December.

It was moved and carried to end the 1920 circuit in Memphis if they desired it.

It was suggested that the secretary write to Mr. Onderdonk, New York City that the Society would like to exhibit in the Dallas, Texas State Fair as a body for 1921, and that individuals would exhibit there this year and that he, if he could, should group them if possible. Refreshments were served and meeting adjourned.

Motion seconded and carried

Signed,
Walter Ufer
Secretary & Treasurer.

Minutes of the Meeting held October 7th, 1920
of the Taos Society of Artists
at Blumenschein's Residence in Taos, 7:15 P.M.

The president opened the meeting at 7:15 P.M. Members Couse, Phillips, Sharp, Higgins, Dunton, Blumenschein and Ufer were present. Members Henri, Rolshoven, Groll and Berninghaus were absent.

The reports and minutes of the secretary and treasurer of the last meeting, August 24th, were read and approved.

It was suggested that the secretary write to Mr. J. S. Clatsworthy, Estes Park, Colorado, art dealer and see if we could exhibit our 1921 circuit there instead of Hardy's at Colorado Springs.

It was suggested to write to Hug & Sarachek, Kansas City, Missouri and find out from him what he considered the best season for displaying art in his territory.

It was suggested to write to Gage in Cleveland, Ohio.

It was suggested to write to the Mohr Galleries, Toledo, Ohio.

It was motioned, seconded and carried that the ruling made at the meeting of July 12th, 1920 on sizes of paintings for our

1921 circuit be amended so as to read, "not over 1300 square inches."

The secretary made announcement of that the Kingore Galleries of New York City would receive any addresses of possible clients at the exhibition in November and also that the secretary would again give this out in his final notice to the members.

Meeting adjourned.

Carried

Signed,
Walter Ufer
Secretary & Treasurer

1921

Report of the Secretary
Taos Society of Artists
1920 and 1921

The Society's membership at present consists of nine active and two associate members whose names are as follows: Active—Berninghaus, Blumenschein, Couse, Dunton, Higgins, Sharp, Phillips, Rolshoven and Ufer. Associates—Henri and Groll. Honorary—Springer & Hewett.

The present administration has had charge of the Taos Society of Artists exactly for one year, for it was July 12th, 1920 that they were elected to take charge of the affairs of the Society.

After they agreed to accept the offices to which they were elected the president, E. L. Blumenschein, immediately laid out his plans for the year of which the exhibition circuit constructed the main thing.

It was his idea that the Society should grow and expand so long as we had other excellent and standard artists in nearby towns, and explained that the Society could benefit vastly by such proceedings. He, therefore, laid the names of three excellent artists before the members of the Society and asked us to vote an invitation to these gentlemen to exhibit one or two paintings with us in our commonly called 1921 circuit. After fair discussion this was agreed to by the members and voted for, and this invitation was given personally to the three artists living and working in Santa Fe. They agreed to abide by our rules and four paintings were sent in by the three invited.

The names of these artists are Sloan, Nordfeldt and Davey.

The next move that our president suggested was to get the Taos Society of Artists exhibition for the first time during their existence in a Fifth Avenue gallery of New York City. This, after much writing, was accomplished by the secretary.

The Taos Society of Artists then opened their 6th Annual Exhibition at the Kingore Galleries, 668 Fifth Avenue, New York City, November 15th, 1920, and with very great success among the people there. Dr. Christian Brinton was the lecturer there for the opening event, and which was very well attended by the people.

The newspapers of New York City, even the magazines, took up our exhibition and did it great justice. They gave due credit to each man mentioned.

The exhibitors were and are Berninghaus, Blumenschein, Couse, Davey, Dunton, Henri, Higgins, Groll, Nordfeldt, Phillips, Sharp, Sloan and Ufer. Thirteen in all. After the New York exhibit Mr. Groll dropped out. The circuit had to be idle in New York for a month on account of beginning so early as November, December being a Christmas month with the dealers, it was very difficult to place the exhibition. However, at the first of the year the circuit started for Dayton, Ohio and was followed by Toledo, Chicago, St. Louis, Kansas City, Salt Lake City and is now in Denver. It will be shipped and is booked for San Diego, San Francisco, Honolulu, Santa Fe and will then disband.

No sales can be reported so far which [is] probably due to the conditions of the country at the present time—though there is hope.

After the secretary took charge he took charge of the old 1920 circuit while it was in Colorado Springs, and after September 1st., had it shipped to Des Moines and Nashville.

Two sales were made, one each in Des Moines and Nashville, and succeeded in getting Nashville to pay all expenses of shipments of paintings back to the artists' addresses.

The president next thought it good to have a biographical

data sheet printed and this was voted on and accepted. This cost the Society $45.00 and as the treasury did not hold that amount it was decided to assess each member $3.00 and which was collected.

It was next agreed upon by the Governing Board to assess each sale made 1% of the selling price, and our member E. I. Couse is the first to pay 1%, having made a sale in Nashville.

The secretary has up to and before this date managed the affairs of the Society, the circuit, and all business transactions so that the new secretary has but to fall in and follow up the work. The final exact dates with San Diego, San Francisco, Honolulu and Santa Fe are not made yet, but the exhibition is assured.

The main idea which the secretary during his work received was as follows, and which this officer lays before the members as an urgent suggestion for the future.

Our work though always well liked by the press, the dealers and the public, and has been in demand over the entire country, it was felt that the invited names were an asset to our already good collection. Therefore, the secretary suggests *growth*.

It was very difficult to get our exhibition into New York and Chicago among the dealers because our past exhibitions were not of high enough standard. In passing through these two cities the secretary received verbally from dealers and artists alike what he scented through the mails.

Therefore, the secretary advises if we wish to succeed to take into our cover in the future those who deliver good and standard work of whatever *Ism* and who do just as much to help the Southwest a step along and to further America's name in Art.

It is further suggested that the Society should aim to keep its treasury as full as possible. We must bear in mind that in this new era money is more necessary than before. Members resent being assessed continually for we know how hard it was to collect the last assessment. Dances, costume parties and such like could be given continually throughout the year in Taos under the auspices of an entertainment committee and this could help keep our treasury in working order and would easily lessen the work of the future officers.

It is urgent to keep in mind that the country and its people demand more and more of us as we get older and better established—but this also demands money to do such with. We are now well established with the people urging us to do big and great things. We have not accomplished this yet for we must set all of our shoulders together to keep abreast with the pace that others are setting who are in the same field to further the name of America.

Approved &
Carried

Faithfully submitted,
The Secretary.
Walter Ufer

Report of T. S. of A.
Annual Meeting 7/12/21

This meeting was called at the residence of E. L. Blumenschein for 8 P.M. Was opened by the president, Mr. E. L. Blumenschein at 8:15 P.M. Members present were Berninghaus, Couse, Dunton, Higgins, Phillips, Sharp, Blumenschein and Ufer.

Minutes of meeting held October 7, 1920 were read, approved and carried. Last annual secretary & treasurer report read, approved and carried. Thereupon Mr. Dunton was asked to place his story which he had written according to the magazines he mentioned. President read his report which was carried.

Thereupon Mr. John Sloan, Mr. Randall Davey and Mr. B. J. O. Nordfeldt were elected associates.

Mr. Herbert Dunton was placed chairman of the Entertainment Committee; Higgins and Berninghaus to assist. It was decided to give an annual dance in the town of Taos which proved a great success.

Then the election of officers took place and E. L. Blumenschein was reelected as president, Walter Ufer was reelected as secretary & treasurer and Higgins reelected as member of the Governing Board.

Thereupon various letters were read to assure the members that the circuit was properly proceeding.

Meeting adjourned.

Approved &
Carried

Faithfully submitted,
Walter Ufer
Sec'y & Treasurer.

Report of the Entertainment Committee
of the Taos Society of Artists
on the Dance given by the Society
on the night of July 27th, '21

Following the meeting of the Taos Society of Artists at which an Entertainment Committee was formed this committee commenced work at once on the first entertainment to be given by the Society—a dance at Miramon's Hall on the night of July 27th, 1921.

Two meetings of the committee were called by the chairman, both of which were held at the residence of Mr. O. E. Berninghaus.

At the first meeting of the Entertainment Committee the chairman appointed Mr. Berninghaus in charge of all publicity connected with the dance. Mr. Higgins was put in charge of the tickets and their distribution. The chairman allotted to himself the duties of procuring the hall and the supervision of its preparation for the affair and also to procuring as good music for the occasion as was possible. Suggestions in the line of a novelty as an entertainment feature and as a "drawing card" were discussed. Mr. Berninghaus' proposal of a dance by a few of the Taos Indians was dropped—principally due to the necessary expense it would incur.

Following this meeting Mr. Berninghaus at once made several attractive signs advertising the dance which were immediately put in prominent windows about the Plaza, at Ranchos, Questa and at Red River. Handbills he also had printed which were sent by him to various artists in Santa Fe, the Santa Fe *New Mexican*, and were also distributed about town. Mr. Higgins had tickets printed and saw that they were distributed to the different members of the organization and an ample number left at the Rio Grande Drug Store.

The second and last meeting of the Entertainment Committee held before the dance was held at Mr. Berninghaus' on the Monday evening preceding the affair. The chairman announced his appointment of Mr. Walter Ufer as floor director for the occasion. This appointment was sanctioned by the committee. This second meeting was called principally to discuss the advisability of a proposal by Mr. Higgins that, as an entertainment feature, a "raffle" be "pulled off" with a humorous climax following the Grand March. His suggestion was—briefly—to lead the gathering to believe that a painting was to be "raffled" free of any extra charge (each ticket holder upon entering the hall was to receive a number which entitled him or her to one "chance") but in place of the supposed canvas a certain decrepit, maimed and forlorn dog-about-town was to be presented to the fortunate individual drawing the lucky number. Mr. Higgins' proposal was, in the main, accepted with enthusiasm. Due to the inhuman phase in view of the dog's physical condition and also to his viciousness the dog was replaced by a pig. Mr. Higgins was appointed as a committee of one to see this feature of the program through.

Mr. Berninghaus made arrangements with Mrs. Cheetham whereby refreshments of ice cream, cake and punch would be served. This was decidedly a desirable feature of the occasion.

The dance in question came off on the night of July 27th, 1921 and every detail worked out as planned. The success—socially—of this first entertainment given by the Taos Society of Artists can be judged by those members who were present.

The gross income derived from the entertainment, the disbursements and net profit are as follows—

Gross proceeds	$117.00	
Disbursements		
Music		$25.00
Rent of Hall		$15.00
Printing of Tickets & Handbills		$ 9.50
Dancing Wax		$ 1.40
Decorations for Pig		.70
Card board		$ 1.00
War Tax		$11.00
Total Disbursements		$64.10
Net Profit	$52.90	

In submitting this report of the Entertainment Committee the chairman desires to thank Mr. Berninghaus for the time he gave to and the efficiency with which he handled the publicity end of the committee's duties. He also wished to record his thanks to Mr. Higgins for his "prize pig" idea (which proved such a wonderful "hit") and for the time and thought he gave this feature which insured its success.

The chairman also desires to thank Mr. Ufer for his active

campaign in the sale of tickets and for the interest and efficiency he displayed in the capacity of floor manager.

The costume ball contemplated for September 1921 was abandoned as inadvisable by the Entertainment Committee.

Hoping the entertainment given—and results attained—will meet with the approval of the Society, this report is respectfully submitted.[14]

W. Herbert Dunton
Chairman

1922

Report of the Secretary and Treasurer:
Taos Society of Artists—1921–1922

The Society's membership at present consists of eight active, five associate, and two honorary members. They are as follows: Active—Berninghaus, Blumenschein, Couse, Dunton, Higgins, Sharp, Phillips, Rolshoven and Ufer. Associate—Davey, Groll, Henri, Nordfeldt, Sloan. Honorary—Mr. Frank Springer and Dr. Edgar L. Hewett.

The present administration has had charge of the affairs of the Taos Society of Artists exactly for two years to date, having been reelected last July 12th, 1921. After they agreed to accept their offices another year the president Mr. E. L. Blumenschein laid out his plans for the year of which the circuit exhibition constituted the main idea. This 1922 circuit is now on exhibition in Denver and Colorado Springs and will remain there until September first. To date three paintings have been sold out of this circuit, and we look forward to selling many more before the close. This circuit began in Baltimore last December and was exhibited in Pittsburgh, Detroit, Indianapolis, St. Louis, and Kansas City.

Our 1921 circuit started in New York and travelled all the way to Honolulu and on its return was exhibited in San Francisco and Wichita, Kansas. Out of this circuit three paintings were sold.

Much to our regret we find that Herbert Dunton has resigned from our strong little Society. He no doubt has his reasons, and the secretary suggests to not let up and elect a still stronger man in his place.

It has been a pleasure to serve as your secretary and treasurer and this pleasure was largely added to by noticing that our Society is very much in demand throughout the country.

I believe that as an officer I have been in closer contact with the outside relative to the business of the Society than the other members and from my observations made would suggest to hold still closer together and work much harder than before in order to keep the Society in its rightful place and that as the foremost art organization of the United States.

Therefore elect still stronger men as members.

Approved &	Faithfully submitted,
Carried.	Walter Ufer
Ufer	The Secretary.

8th. Annual Meeting Minutes
Annual Meeting, July 12th 1922
T. S. of A.

The meeting was called to order by the president Mr. E. L. Blumenschein at 8:25 P.M. Members present were Berninghaus, Blumenschein, Couse, Phillips, Sharp & Ufer.

The report of the annual meeting of July 12th 1921 was read, approved & carried.

The report of the secretary and treasurer was read, approved & carried.

Letters about the 1922 circuit showing where the exhibit is located and where it will proceed to . . . were read. Letter of American Fed. of Arts asking for a group exhibition was read. It was by vote decided to write the Federation that individual members would exhibit if they were asked, but that at the present [nothing] could be sent . . . but would be considered in the future.

Report from Herbert Dunton as chairman of the Entertainment Committee was read, approved & carried.

Thereafter Mr. Dunton's resignation was read, and it was decided to accept his resignation.

Birger Sandzen, artist of Lindsborg, Kansas, was elected unanimously associate member.

Gustave Baumann, artist of Santa Fe, was elected [associate] member unanimously. Both must be notified and both are to pay dues.

Then the election of officers took place. Walter Ufer was elected president. O. E. Berninghaus was elected secretary and treasurer. Bert Phillips was elected the third member of the Governing Board.

Mr. Dunton must be notified of our acceptance of his resignation.

E. L. Blumenschein was appointed chairman of the Entertainment Committee with the right to choose his assistants. It was decided to start arrangements for a grand dance.

Meeting adjourned at 11 P.M.

Walter Ufer

Berny:
Please mail reports to all the associate members and Frank Springer, Santa Fe, N.M. & Dr. Edgar L. Hewett, Santa Fe. Associates pay $5.00 dues excepting Sloan.

[The following letter was written by Blumenschein three days after the 1922 annual meeting.]

July 15, 1922

Sec'y Taos Soc. of Artists
Dear Mr. Berninghaus:

At the recent meeting of the Society at my residence no action was taken thanking me for my services during my two years in office. I made no melodramatic display to indicate that I had been working for your interests, but there had been considerable to do, especially at the beginning of each season.

The morning after the meeting I told Mrs. Blumenschein

that the Society had passed a resolution thanking her for the pains she had taken to see that there was some refreshment at each meeting during the two years. Of course, no such resolution was passed, but I would not have her think that to be the case.

I was very careful to see that the Society recognized the labors of the secretary, but the entire bunch including the secretary forgot there had been a president.

I have waited two days since the meeting hoping someone might have noticed the error, but as no remark or communication has been made on this subject I do not feel inclined to be of further service to the organization.

Mr. Dunton told Couse that his reason for resigning was because he did not care to belong to a society in which the sec'y referred to the president as a "bald-headed S.B." Couse repeated this to me with pleasure; Dunton told me he had it straight and would stand pat on it: the sec'y said he didn't remember having made the remark, but he neither denied it nor apologized.

As little events of this nature seem to be gladly spread by some member to the outside world and come back to us *much magnified,* I will appreciate some action of the Taos Society that will remedy this situation.

Until such action is taken officially by the entire body of active members (excepting myself) you may consider me as outside the club.

Sincerely yours,
Ernest L. Blumenschein

1923

The Annual Report of the President of the Taos Society of Artists July 13, 1923

Gentlemen:

The president took his office last year in July and continued the 1921–22 circuit which finished in Santa Fe about October.

Besides this work there was nothing of any note to perform.

The very able secretary, Mr. O. E. Berninghaus, performed his duties to such an extent that I hope a special thanks will be offered him.

The business of the year will no doubt be read by Mr. Berninghaus.

Thanking you & respectfully submitted,

I am yours,

Walter Ufer
President
July 1923

Report of Secretary and Treasurer Taos Society of Artists 1922–1923.

The Society's membership at present consists of eight active, seven associates and two honorary members—they are as follows:

Active: O. E. Berninghaus, E. L. Blumenschein, A.N.A.; E. I. Couse, N.A.; Victor Higgins, A.N.A.; J. H. Sharp; B. G. Phillips; Julius Rolshoven; Walter Ufer, A.N.A.

Associate: Albert Groll, N.A.; Robert Henri, N.A.; B. J. Nordfeldt; John Sloan; Randall Davey; Gustave Baumann; Birger Sandzen.

Honorary: Mr. Frank Springer, Dr. Edgar Hewett.

The report of the secretary consists mainly in an outline of the Society's exhibition circuit, which began in New York City at Howard Young Galleries on November 4, 1922. After showing here two weeks the collection was forwarded to Worcester Art Museum at Worcester, Mass., where it was shown during the month of December, 1922. In January 1923, it was exhibited at the Cleveland Art Museum; in February at Traxel Art Company of Cincinnati, Ohio; March at H. Lieber Company Galleries at Indianapolis, Indiana; April in St. Louis, Noonan-Kocian Galleries; May in Kansas City, Conrad Hug Galleries; June, Cyrus Boutwell Galleries in Denver; July at Boutwell Galleries in Colorado Springs, where it will remain for the tourist summer season and until some other exhibition point is decided upon.

In the collection were twenty-seven canvases representing the following artists: Berninghaus, Blumenschein, Couse, Higgins, Groll, Phillips, Sandzen, Nordfeldt, Sharp and Ufer. Regrets were felt at different points that some members were not represented.

Sales: The first was reported at Cincinnati, a canvas by Couse; at St. Louis four canvases were sold, namely, Couse, Sharp and Berninghaus.

The press, as usual, throughout the country has given us liberal space wherever the collection was shown, and all exhibition points report a good attendance and quite a bit of interest, especially at Worcester and Cincinnati. Both Boutwell galleries of Denver and Colorado Springs were somewhat inclined not to take the show this year but after a little correspondence agreed to try it again this season. The comments of the latter were to the effect that the pictures were too large and prices too high, and beyond the reach of their clientele.

All galleries where the exhibition was held issued special

catalogs; particular mention may be made of the catalog issued by Howard Young Galleries, New York.

It is unnecessary to state that the Society is undoubtedly one of the best known in the United States. It is noted, however, that there is a feeling among some that our traveling exhibition is somewhat commercial, and that we are not showing canvases we are capable of.

Several special meetings were held during the past year at which minor business relative to the Society's affairs were disposed of without mentioning them in detail in this report.

An invitation to become a chapter member of the American Federation of Arts was extended the Society. Acceptance was deferred to the annual meeting and should be considered at that time.

O. E. Berninghaus
Respectfully submitted,
Secretary and Treasurer.

[This is one of several nominations for membership that are preserved in the T.S.A. file. The names of William P. Henderson and Jozef Bakos were crossed out and were not submitted at the meeting.]

May-26-23
We the undersigned hereby nominate for membership in the T.S.A. the following (all of Santa Fe):
Mr. Henderson
Mr. Bakos
Mr. Parsons
Mr. Van Soelen
Signed

Ernest L. Blumenschein
V. Higgins
Walter Ufer

Taos N.M. 7/3-23
Taos Soc. of Artists—
Taos N.M.
We the undersigned hereby nominate Mr. Martin Hennings for membership in the Taos Society of Artists.
O. E. Berninghaus
Walter Ufer

Minutes of Annual Meeting,
Taos Soc. of Artists—7/13-23

The annual meeting of the Taos Soc. of Artists was held July 13th 1923 at studio of O. E. Berninghaus.

Members present—O. E. Berninghaus, E. L. Blumenschein, E. I. Couse, Victor Higgins, Bert Phillips, J. H. Sharp & Walter Ufer.

Secretary's report was read & approved. Treasurer's report showing a balance of 90.72 was read & approved.

President's report was read & approved.

On motion of Mr. Couse, seconded by Mr. Blumenschein, it was recommended that the Society become a member of the American Fed. of Arts—dues of which are 10.00 per annum.

Future exhibition circuit was discussed. It was suggested by Mr. Couse that Waco, Tex. may be interested and that he could correspond with people there and ascertain whether or not this be possible.

The secretary was instructed to correspond with Santa Fe to get their views on the Society exhibition again showing in its museum this fall.

Election of officers—

After numerous ballots Mr. Sharp was elected president. After repeated balloting the office of secretary for the ensuing year brought no definite result.

It was the sense of the meeting to postpone election of officers and proceed with the election of new members.

The names recommended for membership were Sheldon Parsons [and] Van Soelen for associate membership, Martin Hennings for active membership.

Each name was balloted upon & none received the required two-thirds vote to elect them to membership.

Mr. Sharp at this point declared his refusal to accept the presidency and verbally tendered his resignation. This left all offices again vacant and as the hour became late with no encouragement for a solution of this question it was motioned by Mr. Higgins, seconded by Mr. Phillips, that meeting adjourn to reconvene on the evening of July 23rd. Carried.

Continued Session of Annual Meeting,
T.S.A., July 23, 1923

The minutes of the first meeting, adjourned July 13, were read and generally approved. The exception being that Mr. Couse wished it to be understood that the purpose of adjournment was to allow time for the formulation of such amendments to the Constitution & By-laws for presentation at this meeting.

No written notice of any proposed change in the Constitution was presented. However, on motion of Mr. Couse it was unanimously voted to waive written notice of any change and submit at this meeting for consideration or adoption such resolutions as may be presented.

The following resolution offered by Mr. Couse and seconded by Mr. Phillips was carried by a vote of 4 to 2:

"Resolved—that articles four & five of the Constitution & By-laws of the Taos Society of Artists relating to the election of officers be changed to read as follows:

There shall be one officer in the Taos Society of Artists whose duty it shall be to conduct the business of the Society. Each active member shall serve in alphabetical order for one year and that a refusal to serve be considered equivalent to a resignation from the Society unless there be a reason acceptable to the Society."

Motion by Mr. Couse that because of the previous and present service as secretary of the Society Mr. Berninghaus' name be placed last on the alphabetical list.

The secretary was instructed to acquaint Mr. E. L. Blumenschein of the adoption of the resolution effecting the change in the Constitution and to notify him that his name appears next in alphabetical order and that the office mentioned in the resolution is accordingly now in his charge.

On motion of Mr. Higgins, seconded by Mr. Phillips, the following resolution amending the Constitution of the Society was adopted:

"Any active member absenting himself for one year and ceasing active participation in the Society shall be classed to associate membership but automatically is reinstated upon his return to qualifications of active membership."

There being no further business the meeting was adjourned.

O. E. Berninghaus
Sec'y

July 24, 1923

Sec'y, T.S.A.
Taos, N.M.
Dear Mr. Berninghaus,

Yours of July 24th rec'd.

The end of your amendment reads as follows: "—unless there be a reason acceptable to the Society."

I shall have to ask you to consider my reason for declining the secretaryship.

It is that it will be impossible for me to undertake the duties of a secretary for two societies, as it is an office, as you well know, that requires a great sacrifice of one's time.[15]

I shall not attend this meeting, thus allowing you to discuss the matter openly between yourselves.

Kindly advise me of the result.

With best wishes,
Sincerely yours,
Ernest L. Blumenschein

Minutes of the Meeting,
Taos Soc. of Artists, July 31–'23

Members present—Berninghaus, Couse, Higgins, Sharp, Phillips, Ufer.

Minutes of the meeting of July 23 were read and after several objections by Mr. Higgins as to their accuracy was finally accepted as read.

Letter from Dr. Edgar Hewett of the Santa Fe Museum, inviting our Society to exhibit at the Museum during the Fiesta early in September, was read. It was agreed, if possible, to send our circuit exhibition now at Colorado Springs to Santa Fe and for the secretary to arrange details with the authorities at that place (Santa Fe).

A letter from Mr. E. L. Blumenschein was read. This was a reply to letter advising him that in accordance with the amendment to [the] Constitution & By-Laws adopted at the annual meeting of July 21 [actually, the continued session of the annual meeting on July 23], the office of secretary is now in his charge. In Mr. Blumenschein's excuse he declared his inability to serve because of his secretaryship of another organization and felt it impossible to give his time to two organizations.

In view of the fact that he was conscious of his obligations to our Society in that he had on several occasions promised to accept the duties and assume charge beginning last annual meeting and because of the penalties contained in the Constitution, the question of his excuse became a matter of lengthy and at times heated discussion, and at a point when the question was about to be presented to the Society for formal vote, Mr. Ufer, the chairman, left the meeting in an impulse and declared himself *not present*. This left five members present, namely Berninghaus, Couse, Higgins, Sharp & Phillips.

In Mr. Ufer's absence, Mr. Berninghaus was asked to act as chairman and placed the following question before the Society:

"Those in favor of accepting Mr. Blumenschein's excuse will please say 'I'"—No response.

"Those in favor of not accepting Mr. Blumenschein's excuse will please say 'I'"—3 "I's" responded.

Accordingly, Mr. Blumenschein's excuse as outlined in his letter refusing the office of secretary was not accepted.

Mr. Couse's name appearing next in alphabetical order to accept the office, was declared the secretary and not having any excuse to offer took charge immediately.

After some discussion about [the] next exhibition circuit and other matters of lesser importance, the meeting adjourned.[16]

1924

Report of E. Irving Couse, Official of the Taos Society of Artists, year 1923–4

The annual circuit exhibition of the Taos Society of Artists opened Jan. 2nd 1924 at the Ferargil Galleries, N.Y. There were 29 pictures of various sizes in the exhibition, 12 of our members being represented. One picture by Rolshoven was sold. During Feb., the exhibition was shown at the John Hanna Galleries in Detroit; March at the Traxel Galleries, Cincinnati; April, Noonan-Kocian, St. Louis; May, Hug Galleries, Kansas City; June, Dow Galleries, Denver; July & August it will be shown at the Francis Galleries, Estes Park; Aug. 25 to Sept. 14th at the Museum of Santa Fe; Sept. 18 to 28th at the International Fair at El Paso, after which it was the intention to disband this exhibition. I am, however, at present in communication with the Association of Western Museum Directors for the formation of a Pacific Coast circuit after El Paso & have no doubt it will be arranged to send the circuit there after which the paintings will, I hope, be delivered without charge to the individual artists.

Although my office expires tonight I will, as I have the affairs of the present circuit in hand, with the consent of my successor, continue to conduct it until its disbandment.

Although this year's exhibit has been tolerably well received, I feel that in the future stronger efforts should be made to strengthen it by the members sending their best works. We have achieved an enviable reputation in the past which requires greatly increased effort to sustain.

The present membership of the Society consists of 6 active, 8 associate & 2 honorary members.

There is a movement on foot by an admirer of the Indian in Washington, D.C. to have an exhibition of Indian paintings with several prizes this fall in either the Corcoran Gallery or the Smithsonian Institution, & although nothing definite has yet been settled, I am in hopes something to our benefit will accrue & am working on this matter to that end.

Respectfully submitted,
E. Irving Couse
Approved
July 12, '24
EIC

Expenses of Taos Society of Artists, 1923–4

1923		
Aug 6	Stamps & stationery	2.50
" 8	Dues, American Federation of Arts	10.00
" 25	500 letterhead envelopes & P.P. Kutterer Jansen Printing Co. . . . . St. Louis, Mo.	20.27
Nov 20	Stamps	1.00
Dec 7	" & postcards	.60
Jan 24	A.P. & S. [Artists' Packing & Shipping Co.] unpacking & delivery to Ferargil	17.75
Feb	" packing & shipping to Detroit	43.40
May 16	Dues, American Fed. of Arts, Wash. D.C.	10.00
Jun 15	Stamps	.50
		106.02

Funds of the Taos Society of Artists, 1923–4
Receipts

Aug 2	Bal. turned over by O. E. Berninghaus	90.72
" 7	Dues. E. I. Couse, 58 W. 57, N.Y.	5.00
" 10	" O. E. Berninghaus, 7703 Walinca Terrace, Clayton, St. Louis Co., Mo.	5.00
" 11	" J. H. Sharp, Taos, N. Mex.	5.00
" 17	Dues. Bert Phillips, " "	5.00
" 18	" Birger Sandzen, Lindsborg, Kan.	5.00
Sept 25	" Walter Ufer, Taos, N. Mex.	5.00
Oct 13	Commission, J. H. Sharp, Santa Fe sale	3.00

Nov 20	Dues. John Sloan, 88 Washington Place, N.Y.	5.00
Dec 3	" J. Rolshoven, 140 W. 57, N.Y.—1922–3	10.00
Oct 15	" Victor Higgins, Taos, N. M.	5.00
Dec 19	" B. J. O. Nordfeldt, Santa Fe, N. Mex.	5.00
Jan 31, '24	" Robt. Henri, 10 Gramercy Park, N.Y.	5.00
Apr 14, '24	Commission, Rolshoven sold Ferargil 1%	3.50
	Total receipts	157.22
	Total expenses	106.02
	Bal. July 12, '24	51.20

Delinquent members for dues 1924

A. L. Groll	5.00—Pd. Oct. 1924	
Randall Davey	5.00	Pd. May 20, 1925
Gus Baumann	5.00	Pd. Oct. 1924
July 12, '24 total	15.00	

Approved
July 12, '24
EIC

Taos N.M. June 29-24

To the Taos Society of Artists—

The name of Mr. E. Martin Hennings is submitted and recommended for membership in the Society by the undersigned.

O. E. Berninghaus
Bert G. Phillips

Elected

Taos, N.M. June 29-24

To the Taos Society of Artists
The name of Miss Catharine C. Critcher is submitted and recommended for membership in the Society by the undersigned.

O. E. Berninghaus
Bert G. Phillips

Elected

Taos, N.M. June 29-24

To the Taos Society of Artists
The name of Mr. W. Herbert Dunton is submitted and recommended for membership in the Society by the undersigned.

O. E. Berninghaus
Bert G. Phillips

Withdrawn

Minutes of Annual Meeting of the Taos Society of Artists, July 12th, 1924

The 10th annual meeting of the T.S.A. was held at the studio of E. Irving Couse on July 12th, 1924. The meeting was called to order at 8:30 P.M. E. I. Couse, the officer of the Society, occupying the chair. Members present—O. E. Berninghaus, E. I. Couse, B. G. Phillips, J. H. Sharp, & Walter Ufer.

The minutes of the last meeting held July 31, '23 were read & approved.

Report of the officer regarding circuit exhibition & matters of general interest read & approved. Financial report showing a balance of funds in the treasury of $51.20 read & approved.

Election of new members.—
Miss Catharine Critcher & Mr. E. Martin Hennings were unanimously elected to active membership.[17] The name of W. Herbert Dunton was withdrawn from nomination after a lengthy discussion during which it developed that it was the sense of the meeting that Mr. Dunton's previous resignation from the Society was due to the fact that he had refused to consider an election as secretary & an election to membership at the present time would be inadvisable until he would agree to fulfill what was considered a former obligation.

Owing to the absence of Victor Higgins, the new official for the coming year, no new business was discussed & the meeting adjourned at 10 o'clock.

E. Irving Couse

Minutes—Special Meeting held Sept. 19th
at the Home of B. Phillips,
All Active Members Being Present

This meeting was called for the purpose of acting according to the Constitution on the excuse presented by Mr. Higgins for his inability on account of illness to undertake the position of officer of the Society which in rotation fell to him for the year 1924–5. Mr. Higgins' excuse was accepted as satisfactory to the Society with the understanding that he would serve the following year. Mr. Phillips being next in order presented also an excuse of illness & was also excused.

Mr. Sharp being next in order & having no excuse was declared the officer of the Society for the year 1924.

The new officer was instructed to arrange the year's circuit exhibition to start in Oklahoma City & include the winter months in that vicinity & the summer months in Kansas, Colorado, & New Mexico.

Meeting adjourned at 9:30 P.M.

E. Irving Couse
Acting Secretary

[In 1924, J. H. Sharp, in his capacity as secretary, had the following letter of instructions printed to be sent to all members of the Society.]

Taos Society of Artist[s]
Taos, New Mexico
Exhibition Circuit Season 1924–5

The 1924–5 exhibition circuit will open at Ft. Worth, Texas, Nov. 10th.

We have planned to make this by far the most representative collection ever assembled by the Society and we are relying upon you to select your very best canvases for this circuit.

The enclosed tags, one for each work, should be properly and plainly filled out and attached to back of frame and a duplicate should be sent in advance as early as possible to the secretary, so that catalog may be printed in time for the opening day.

Only three works will be accepted from each member, and largest canvas must not exceed 1300 square inches in size.

All frames should be carefully chosen and in good condition and in accordance with recent Express Company rulings, glass should be eliminated.

It has been found impractical to make satisfactory arrangements for insurance and it is therefore suggested that each member give this his individual attention for such works as he will exhibit.

While the collection is on tour through the country, it will as far as possible be shown at the most prominent gallery or museum in each city and handled by experienced people, thus lessening to a great extent possible loss or damage.

Our past exhibitions have attracted a great deal of attention wherever shown, and the press has given us endless space in its columns.

Sales also have been encouraging and with the new collection which is expected to be stronger and better than ever, we have a better season, artistically and otherwise.

Do not fail to send titles and prices of each work to secretary as soon as possible.

Photos of paintings should accompany this for press use.

There is also to be an illustrated catalogue to be used on

the whole circuit, and it is important not to overlook the photos.

Ship pictures by express, charges collect,—value $500 on each box to Sam M. Yunt, Ft. Worth, Texas.

Pictures must be there by Nov. 5th.

J. H. Sharp
Secretary
Taos, New Mexico

1925

Taos, N. Mex., July 11th, 1925

Report of the 1923–24 Circuit Exhibition of the Taos Society of Artists

At the close of the eastern circuit, 1923–24, which included New York, Detroit, St. Louis, Cincinnati, Denver, Kansas City, Estes Park, Santa Fe, & El Paso, the exhibition was turned over to the Western Ass'n of Art Museum Directors with headquarters at Los Angeles who arranged a Pacific Coast circuit which included San Diego, Oakland, Seattle, University of Oregon at Eugene, Medford, Oregon, University of Montana at Missoula, Fresno State Teacher's College at Fresno, & Seymour, Indiana, from which place it was returned free of all expense to the individual artists in June 1925.

E. Irving Couse
Sec. 1923–4

List of Members, T.S.A., 1924–1925

Active Members:
O. E. Berninghaus, 7703 Walinca Terrace, Clayton, St. Louis Co., Mo.
E. Irving Couse, (winter) 58 W. 57th St., N.Y., (summer) Taos, N. Mex.
Bert Phillips, Taos, N. Mex.
Catharine Critcher, 3 St. Mathew's Alley, Washington, D.C.
E. Martin Hennings, 4 E. Ohio St., Chicago, Ill., (summer) Taos.
J. H. Sharp, 1481 Carson St., Pasadena, Cal., (summer) Taos, N. Mex.
Victor Higgins, Taos, N. Mex.
Walter Ufer, Taos, N. Mex.

Associate Members:
B. J. O. Nordfeldt, Santa Fe, N. Mex.
Julius Rolshoven, 140 West 57th St., N.Y. City.
Birger Sandzen, Lindsborg, Kansas.
Randall Davey, Santa Fe, N. Mex.
John Sloan, 88 Washington Place, N.Y. City.
Robert Henri, 10 Gramercy Park, N.Y. City.
Gustave Baumann, Santa Fe, N. Mex.
A. L. Groll, 222 West 59th St., N.Y. City.

Honorary Members:
Dr. Hewett, Museum of Santa Fe, N. Mex.
Mr. Frank Springer, " "

Official Report of the T.S.A., Year 1924–5

All dues paid up. Delinquents came through after repeated duns—except Henri & Sloan. These two probably drop out by ignoring requests for dues & pictures.

Exhibition consisting of 27 paintings turned over to Sam M. Yunt for circuit of the Southwest, opening in Ft. Worth in Nov. Yunt's letters make better report than I can, and think all members should hear or read them.[18]

A sale of a Phillips to a college in Wichita has not been paid. A late letter says he can make satisfactory arrangements for all (check for 200 rec'd since above).

General complaint from Traxel last year, several personal letters and talks, and Yunt, say prices are too high for sales on circuit outside of N.Y. & Chicago.

If sales are desired, I would advise new pictures, modest in size & price, attractively framed, with a light shadow or protection box of same color as frame. This simplifies packing & handling and saves your frames!

If publicity is desired I would suggest going back to the

museums and art associations and make a larger & more worthwhile show. So many refusals on account of expense, it is going to be more & more difficult in future to get the dealers to handle. The other alternative is to dig in your pockets for transportation.

Exhibit shipped to Denver June 9th, short four pictures, 2 Rolshoven, 1 Couse, 1 Sharp. Letters will explain. It reached Denver too late for their regular summer exhibition, so they turned it over to Boulder & from there to Estes Park, & after that, Denver Museum. I suggest it be distributed from Denver, as Santa Fe does not want it this year.

The Central Ill. Federation of Art Associations seems the most promising field for next circuit. They can cover three to four months, giving the sec. ample time to arrange future dates. Yunt will take it for the Kansas City Ex. but not on circuit.

If you want to start from the East again you will have to put up the very strongest exhibition the Society is capable of, and of an original character or the critics will turn you down. So many "one man" and dealer shows throughout the country, the Society will have hard work to hold the interest of the public and the enviable position and reputation they have.

It is well worth while to go on, even if in the end you must pay something more, for I'm sure you have all felt the indirect value of the immense publicity the Society has received.

Only trouble "happens"—we've got to get out & hustle to make things go.

J. H. Sharp

[The archives of the Museum of New Mexico do not contain minutes of the annual meeting of the Taos Society of Artists for 1925; however, the rough notes transcribed on the next page appear to have been taken at that meeting.]

July 12

Berninghaus, Couse, Hennings, Phillips, Ufer, Sharp, Higgins present.

Sec. report read and approved.

1923–24 sec. reported the final closing of his circuit—approved.

The new ex. officer automatically succeeds the 1924–25 sec. and accepts with pleasure [?].

New business:

Motion made and seconded to prepare an instructive article . . . Various members agree . . . in notes to be written later [?].

1926

[The following is a transcription of undated handwritten notes. However, they appear to be notes for the secretary's report for 1926.]

All dues have been paid except Ufer, Davey, Sloan, Henri, Baumann & Groll. Henri and Sloan are delinquent from 1924–25. Former sec. reports that Henri & Sloan did not respond to repeated duns or requests for pictures—which indicates a desire to drop out.

Bills were sent to Ufer, Davey, Baumann and Groll only once. Their failure to remit is probably due to oversight.

The exhibition was turned over to the . . . Illinois Federation of Women's Clubs and was kept in circulation in Illinois and Springfield, Mo. until April or May and was sent to . . . Denver where it is at present.

They want it at a later date and can arrange another exhibit or two—unless the members prefer to have the pictures returned to Taos.

Minutes of Meeting T.S.A. 7/12/26

Members present Berninghaus, Adams, Couse, Critcher, Groll, Higgins, Phillips, Sharp, Ufer.

Principal discussion was in regard to placing future exhibitions where guarantee of at least one sale would be made.

Motion made by Mr. Higgins to write Federation of American Art that sale of one painting must be guaranteed at each exhibition place. Motion seconded by Mr. Ufer. Carried.

Motion by Mr. Berninghaus, seconded by Mr. Couse, that T.S.A. [pay] for boxing Rolshoven's picture. Carried.

Motion that T.S.A. pay expense for return of 1925 circuit pictures, made by Mr. Couse, seconded by Phillips. Carried.

Mr. Berninghaus made the motion, seconded by Mr. Ufer, that while the (3′ × 3′) should remain, an exception should be made to members desiring to exhibit only one large picture not to exceed 40″ × 50″. Carried.

Mr. Ufer motioned to table the matter of arranging circuit until a later meeting. Seconded by Mr. Couse. Carried.

Mr. Ufer made the motion to make the election of Kenneth Adams unanimous, seconded by Mr. Couse. Carried.

Mr. Couse motioned to adjourn, seconded by Mr. Ufer. Carried.

[The minutes of the 1926 annual meeting represent the last document in the files of the Taos Society of Artists. The final act of this organization—their meeting in March 1927, at which time the Society disbanded—was not recorded.

After a meteoric beginning, the Society at the end quietly faded into history. The minutes of the 1926 meeting foretell the demise of the Society. At that meeting the "principal discussion was in regard to placing future exhibitions where guarantee of at least one sale would be made," a stipulation that strongly suggests a problem with lagging sales on the circuit. In addition, "Mr. Ufer motioned to table the matter of arranging circuit until a later meeting." The passage of this motion is very significant when one remembers that the primary purpose of the Society was to sell paintings by means of an annual circuit.

The records of the Taos Society of Artists document a period of creative excellence in northern New Mexico that has assumed legendary proportions. The facts about the birth, life, and death of the Society do not in any way detract from the romantic image that has developed through the years; rather, the contrast between fact and romanticism leads to a better understanding of the complexity of the image of an art colony in Taos. In the history of the Taos Society of Artists, fact is stranger than fiction; truth is more interesting than legend.]

Notes

Introduction

1. Van Deren Coke, *Taos and Santa Fe: The Artist's Environment, 1882–1942* (Albuquerque: University of New Mexico Press, 1963), pp. 23–24, 119.

2. Laura Bickerstaff, *Pioneer Artists of Taos* (Denver: Sage Books, 1955), p. 38.

3. Blanche C. Grant, *When Old Trails Were New* (Chicago: The Rio Grande Press, 1963), p. 269. This book was originally published in 1934 by The Press of the Pioneers. The 1914 date was also used by Kenneth M. Adams some years later ("Los Ocho Pintores," *New Mexico Quarterly* 21 [Summer 1951]: 147.)

4. Ernest L. Blumenschein, "The Taos Society of Artists," *The American Magazine of Art* 8 (September 1917): 451.

5. Patricia Janis Broder, *Taos: A Painter's Dream* (Boston: New York Graphic Society, 1980), pp. 9–10, 290.

6. Broder, *Taos: A Painter's Dream*, p. 10, 290.

7. Bickerstaff, *Pioneer Artists of Taos*, pp. 1–6.

8. Coke, *Taos and Santa Fe*, p. 119.

9. Mary Carroll Nelson, *The Legendary Artists of Taos* (New York: Watson-Guptill, 1980), p. 8. Broder, *Taos: A Painter's Dream*, p. 12.

10. Letter from Mrs. E. Martin Hennings to the author, February 20, 1982.

11. Blanche C. Grant, *When Old Trails Were New* (New York: The Press of the Pioneers, 1934). The photograph of the ten artists faces

page 258. The Rio Grande Press reprint of this book does not contain photographs.

12. Charles E. Lord was a Santa Fe photographer who was active in the years between the World Wars.

13. Kenneth M. Adams, "Los Ocho Pintores," *New Mexico Quarterly* 21 (Summer 1951): 150.

14. John H. McGinnis, "Taos," *Southwest Review* 13 (October 1927): 39–40. Most of this article was reprinted as "It is Written—Taos, Dunton and the Colorado River," *El Palacio* 23 (November 5, 1927): 458.

15. "Fourth Annual Exhibit of the Taos Society of Artists," *El Palacio* 5 (August 10, 1918): 83–90.

Minutes of the Meetings and Related Documents

1. Dr. T. P. Martin was a physician in Taos for many years. His sister, Rose Martin, married Bert Phillips in 1899. Dr. Martin is mentioned numerous times by Mabel Dodge Luhan in her book *Edge of Taos Desert* (New York: Harcourt, Brace and Company, 1937).

2. William Haskell Simpson was born at Lawrence, Kansas, on June 19, 1858, and died in Chicago on June 12, 1933. He began working for the Atchison, Topeka and Santa Fe Railway in 1881 and was the company's advertising manager from 1900 to 1933. Simpson developed the policy of using western paintings in the company's advertising, and was responsible for the formation of the Santa Fe Railway's exceptional art collection. As an example, he purchased seventy-three paintings in 1917, mostly from artists working in Taos and Santa Fe. Irving Couse was Simpson's favorite artist, and Couse paintings were used on Santa Fe Railway calendars almost every year from 1914 to 1938. More information on Simpson can be found in Keith L. Bryant, Jr., "The Atchison, Topeka and Santa Fe Railway and the Development of the Taos and Santa Fe Art Colonies," *Western Historical Quarterly* (October 1978): 436–53, and William H. Simpson Passes On," *Santa Fe Magazine* XXVII, No. 8 (July 1933): 43–44.

Simpson had feelings for the Southwest that went far beyond his business arrangements. In 1929 he published a book of poems entitled *Along Old Trails: Poems of New Mexico and Arizona* (Boston:

Houghton Mifflin). The poems have a strong southwestern flavor, but most deal with loneliness, old age, and death.

3. The letter written to Ufer is reproduced below (courtesy of Steve Good, Rosenstock Arts, Denver, Colorado):

Taos, N.M. 8/15/16

Mr. Walter S. Ufer
San Juan, N.M.

My dear Mr. Ufer:

I have been requested by the members of the Taos Society of Artists to invite you to exhibit three of your recent canvases in our show to be held in Santa Fe the latter part of this month. Pictures are to be sent express collect to Mr. P. A. F. Walter ℅ Amer. School of Archaeology. Title & price on back of picture or sketches—price limit, not lower than $50.00, not over $100,000.00. If you accept please ship not later than Aug. 20th. Hoping you will join us and to see you soon.

Cordially & fraternally yours,
Bert G. Phillips

4. The museum referred to is now the Museum of Fine Arts and is located next to the Palace of the Governors in Santa Fe. The inaugural exhibit was held November 24–December 24, 1917. Paintings were exhibited by Taos Society of Artists members J. H. Sharp, Julius Rolshoven, O.E. Berninghaus, E. Irving Couse, Bert G. Phillips, E. L. Blumenschein, W. Herbert Dunton, Walter Ufer, Victor Higgins, and by future members Robert Henri and E. Martin Hennings.

5. A native of Germany, Paul Alfred Francis Walter was a man of many talents and interests. At various times in his life he was editor of the *Santa Fe New Mexican,* reporter for the New Mexico Supreme Court, postmaster of Santa Fe, founder of *El Palacio,* president of the New Mexico Historical Society, and president of the First National Bank of Santa Fe. At the time that members of the Taos Society of Artists were corresponding with him, Walter was curator of the

Fine Arts Museum (Frank D. Reeve, "Paul A. F. Walter, 1873–1966," *New Mexico Historical Review* XLI, No. 2 [1966]: 165–66).

Gustave Baumann met him during this time and provides a revealing description of Walter in an article entitled "Concerning a Small Untroubled World" (*El Palacio* 78, No. 1 [1972]; also published as a monograph by the Museum of New Mexico Press).

Paul A. F. Walter was the author of several books and monographs, including *The Cities that Died of Fear* (Santa Fe: El Palacio Press, 1931; reprinted by School of American Research) which details a trip he made to the Salinas Pueblos in 1916, accompanied by Walter Ufer, "the Chicago artist."

F. A. Wadleigh was apparently in charge of advertising for the Denver & Rio Grande Railroad.

Gerson Gusdorf was born in Westphalia, Germany, came to the U.S. in 1885, and became successful in the general merchandise business in Taos. He also built and operated the Don Fernando Hotel, and was a patron of many of the Taos artists. See Rebecca Salsbury James, "Gerson Gusdorf, 1869–1951," in *Allow Me to Present 18 Ladies and Gentlemen, and Taos, N.M. 1885–1939* (Taos: El Crepusculo, 1953), pp. 11–13.

Mrs. Pooler of Taos owned the Columbian Hotel.

6. Burt Harwood was an artist who went to Taos in 1916. When he died in 1922, his widow established their home as a public service foundation, the administration of which was transferred to the University of New Mexico in 1936. The Harwood Foundation has a museum, an auditorium, and a library. The museum contains an excellent collection of Taos art, including one of the great masterpieces of the Taos art colony, Victor Higgins's "Winter Funeral."

7. Born November 23, 1865 in Illinois, Dr. Edgar Lee Hewett was to become one of New Mexico's most prominent men of letters, as an archeologist, historian, teacher, writer, and administrator. He was the first president of New Mexico Normal University (New Mexico Highlands), later became director of the School of American Research and Museum of New Mexico in Santa Fe, was professor of archeology and anthropology at the universities of New Mexico and Southern

California, and was one of the founders of the University of New Mexico Press. He died on December 31, 1946. See Paul A. F. Walter, "Edgar Lee Hewett" (necrology): *New Mexico Historical Review* XXII, No. 2 (1947): 190–96.

8. Frank Springer was born at Wapello, Iowa, in 1848. He was admitted to the Iowa bar in 1869, but he had a lifelong interest in paleontology and became a leading authority on crinoids. He moved to Cimarron, New Mexico, in 1873 and served as attorney for the Maxwell Land Grant Company and for the Santa Fe Railway. In 1883 he moved to Las Vegas, New Mexico, and considered it his residence until his death in 1927. It was through his support that the Palace of the Governors was renovated and the Fine Arts Museum was constructed. When Frank Springer died, *El Palacio* carried an eight-page obituary (Vol. 23 [1927]: 315–22) and devoted forty-nine pages to his memorial services (Vol. 23 [1927]: 363–411).

9. The article that so angered Blumenschein's associates was printed under the heading, "Art News From Summer Colonies." The pertinent paragraphs are as follows:

"The readers of the Art News should know that although 2,000 miles away from the Atlantic Ocean, Taos is close to the war, and the artists here have been helping the soldier boys by producing range finders for Camp Funston and Camp Cody, and have received letters expressing great appreciation for the pictures from the commanding officers of the camps. As Chairman of the Range Finder Committee out here, and having had the experience of organizing our war work, I would like the Art News to give space to these few words in relation to this subject. The great fight is a much, very much, bigger cause than the production of beautiful art works.

"I make this statement, which a month ago I would not have thought necessary, because of my experience with painters in the last few weeks. Out here the war work was hardly thought of a month ago. The men were wrapped up in their paintings, in the usual course of a summer's labor, some, in their supreme egotism, feeling that their genius should be unhampered; others in plain selfishness, simply painting because they loved to paint; others producing "pot-boilers" for the winter's market. So when we sent out a call, a private letter to each painter asking him to pledge himself to so many days for one month, and in those days to produce range finders for the Western camps, we began to see that the painter, with a few exceptions was not so anxious to help with his metier, and really sacrifice some of his precious summer days for the benefit of the men who were willing to sacrifice their precious lives. The responses were very slow in coming. One artist said (and it is actually the most outrageous example of egotism I ever encountered) that "he considered his work more important than the war!" Another said he had given this and that and had painted a range finder back East, owned Liberty Bonds and had given generously to the Red Cross, all of which I knew to be true, and now he was going to work for himself until next winter, when he would again help in war work.

"But the war isn't waiting until next winter and the soldiers must be developed. And so I hope that other artists who have reasoned the same way may see this letter, be moved to contribute a range finder, and realize, as Gen. Johnston has said, that it will be of "inestimable value to us in our musketry and machine gun instruction," and realize also that with their hands and brains and talents they are actually of great service in winning the war.

"The Taos painters came around beautifully in the end, and inside of two weeks we had 15 completed canvases, 50 × 70, landscapes and village scenes of France, which are now on their way to help lick the Kaiser."

The next issue of *American Art News* contained three letters related to Blumenschein's article:

That Blumenschein Letter
Taos Artists Protest

Editor American Art News,
Dear Sir:

In order to correct, as nearly as possible, a false impression caused by a letter by Mr. E. L. Blumenschein, published in the American Art News of Sept. 14 last, we would deem it a great favor if you will publish the accompanying letter written by Mr. Blumenschein, which explains itself.

Yours very truly,

E. Irving Couse, W. Herbert Dunton, E. L. Blumenschein, Walter Ufer, Julius Rolshoven, J. H. Sharp and Victor Higgins.

Taos, N.M., Oct. 7, 1918.

Salmagundians Also Protest

Editor American Art News,

Dear Sir:

In your issue of Sept. 14 there appeared a communication from Mr. E. L. Blumenschein of the Taos, N.M., art colony, for which the Salmagundi Club, of which Mr. Blumenschein is a member, wishes to disclaim all responsibility. I fancy that Mr. Blumenschein himself, upon second thought (if, indeed, there can be a second thought, where the first impulse seems to have been so thoughtless), will wish to recall his ungenerous words reflecting upon the good faith and patriotism of his fellow painters.

The Salmagundi Club has been very busy with the painting of so-called "war targets" or "designation charts" for the use of the cantonments in the training of the new men in musketry and machine gun practice. Through our War Service Committee, we have supplied a large number of these "landscape targets" to the various instruction camps, and have received expressions of appreciation from the commanding officers that have greatly encouraged the painters in this unselfish work.

Mr. Blumenschein was designated by our War Service Committee to act for us in forwarding the work among the artists of the Taos colony. It is apparent from the number of indignant protests against his officious comments on his associates received by the Salmagundi Club, that while acting within our discretion in asking him to represent our War Service at Taos, we did not sufficiently appreciate his aptitude for indiscretion.

Very truly yours,
C. M. Fairbanks,
Cor. Sec., Salmagundi Club,

N.Y., Oct. 7, 1918.

Mr. Blumenschein Explains

Editor American Art News,
Dear Sir:

In the Sept. 14 issue of the American Art News you published a letter from Taos signed by myself. Many of the Taos artists have taken great offense at this letter and I very much want to correct their interpretation and to publicly apologize for my blundering words.

Not for one moment had I any intention of conveying the idea that the artists of Taos were not fine, serious men at their art and at all times doing their patriotic "bit" and willing to do more.

But since that campaign for "range-finder" pictures, knowing from generals of the army that these pictures represented the greatest and most useful contributions the artists could make, I was over-zealous in my efforts to impress this knowledge upon artists of all other summer colonies who had not yet painted "range-finders." That was my one big object, to obtain for the soldiers all the pictures possible, and I thought by showing how different artists reasoned before knowing the practical value of the "range-finders," and how, notwithstanding all the many pulls of supporting families in these difficult wartimes, the minute they discovered that they could be of help, they gladly went to work and in two weeks had collected about 20 canvases for the army, I thought that would be proof of the painter's fine willingness to give his talent.

Instead of expressing what was in my mind I clumsily, though innocently, wrote words that some people think malicious and maligning, and I sincerely and ardently hope you will publish this apology that the wrong may be corrected as far as possible.

The artists of the United States are called upon to give not only what the average business man gives in the many branches of war contributions, but in addition, they give free their thousands of posters (of which only a few are chosen), many paintings for "range-finders," and donations to Liberty Loan campaigns, Red Cross and numerous aid societies.

The American artist is certainly giving invaluable help to his government, and I am saddened to think I could have given any other impression.

The many artists of Taos will be particularly indebted for the publication of this note, and needless to say, I will be most grateful.

Sincerely yours,
Ernest L. Blumenschein.

Taos, New Mexico, Oct. 7, 1918.

10. The use of range-finder paintings is discussed in the previous note. Several range-finder paintings were exhibited at the Museum of New Mexico in 1918 and were mentioned in an article in the Museum journal ("Fourth Annual Exhibit of Taos Society of Artists," *El Palacio* 5 [August 10, 1918]: 83–90). Volume 5 (1918) of *El Palacio* contains numerous illustrations of range-finder paintings, including those done by Ufer (p. 148), Sharp (p. 166), Berninghaus (p. 168), Dunton (p. 179), Baumann (p. 188), Blumenschein (p. 279), and Phillips (p. 308). Further information on range-finder paintings may be found in *New Mexico in the Great War* (Lansing B. Bloom, ed., Historical Society of New Mexico Publications in History, Vol. II, November 1927, p. 106–7). This publication contains the following comments: "Mr. Blumenschein on his way to Taos lectured at the New Museum in Santa Fe and explained how these canvases could be utilized in teaching the men how to find the range, how to estimate distances, how to detect 'cover,' how to designate strategical points, and how to make maps. With these landscapes of country in northern France and in Belgium, the student officers also familiarized themselves with the aspects and topography of that portion of Europe." (This quotation may also be found in P. A. F. Walter, "New Mexico in the Great War, IV: 7. Art, Drama, and Literature in War Service," *New Mexico Historical Review* 1 [October 1926]: 417.)

11. The motion picture, containing some exceptional footage of the Taos artists, still exists and can be viewed on appointment at the State Records Center and Archives in Santa Fe. Entitled "Adventures in Kit Carson Land," the movie was filmed in 1917 by El Toro Film Company of Santa Fe, under contract with the State Land Office.

Robert P. Ervien was State Land Commissioner in 1917 and was responsible for the production of the movie. Ervien was born at Ogontz, Pennsylvania, on December 8, 1866 and moved to Clayton, New Mexico, in 1890. He was appointed Territorial Land Commissioner in 1907 by Governor Hagerman and was elected State Land Commissioner upon statehood. Ervien and his wife lived at the Governor's residence while George Curry was governor, and Mrs. Ervien served as hostess at official functions for the divorced Curry (George Curry, *George Curry, 1861–1947, An Autobiography,* ed. H. B. Hening [Albuquerque: University of New Mexico Press, 1958], pp. 206–7, 238).

In 1915 the state legislature passed a bill allowing the State Land Commissioner to expend not more than three percent of his office's budget on publicity designed to increase the value of state lands. Accordingly, a Publicity Bureau was established in the Land Office, but a federal court ruling in October 1917 effectively killed the entire project (*Report of Commissioner of Public Lands,* 1917, pp. 28–32; copy in the Historical Film Collection, State Records Center and Archives).

The Publicity Bureau produced 12,000 feet of film, which was put in storage when the Bureau was abolished. Rediscovered in 1951 in the Capitol, it was thrown out, but was rescued by an alert state employee and eventually 2,500 feet of film were made into a movie.

The theme of the film is an automobile trip through northern New Mexico, but considerable footage is devoted to the Taos artists. A young-looking Buck Dunton is shown petting his dogs as he stands beside the well at what is now the Blumenschein home. In a beautifully composed sequence, Victor Higgins is shown painting a picture of two Pueblo women. Bert Phillips is shown painting a portrait of an Indian man, whereupon Couse, Sharp, and Blumenschein walk up and begin joking with him. Rolshoven is shown painting, Ufer is filmed trading with some Indians, and in a peculiar sequence, a group of artists dressed in costumes for a festival are shown dancing around.

Anyone who has tried to drive through Taos at the height of the tourist season will be interested to learn that the film reveals the traffic in 1917 to have been just as bad—although then most of the traffic consisted of wagons pulled by horses and mules.

In appreciation for his efforts, the Taos artists sent a portfolio of sketches to Robert Ervien on August 28, 1918 (see T.S.A. secretary's report for 1919). Unfortunately, Mr. Ervien did not have long to enjoy the gift, as he died on October 14, 1918 during the great flu epidemic.

12. The exact nature of the Taos Society of Artists' collective objection to Henry C. Balink (his name was spelled Henri Balinck in the secretary's report) is not known. He moved to Taos in 1917, but later settled in Santa Fe. Balink's son, Henry B. Balink, still lives in Santa Fe and was contacted by telephone on February 9, 1983 regarding this incident. Balink said that the effort to deport his father could be attributed to "professional jealousy." He said that his father sold sixteen paintings in eighteen weeks when he first went to Taos and this caused resentment among the artists already there.

A copy of the letter written by the members of the Taos Society of Artists is not contained in the T.S.A. file at the Museum of New Mexico, nor has the letter been located at the National Archives or in the files of the Immigration and Naturalization Service. However, a letter has been located in the National Archives (Record Group 60, Justice Department Central Files 205490) that sheds some light on this issue (it should be noted that this letter was written 3 days *before* the meeting of the Taos Society of Artists during which Balink's status was discussed):

Taos, New Mex.
Oct. 27th 1919

Mr. Palmer
United States Attorney General
Department of Justice
Washington, D.C.

Subject: Henry C. Balink of Amsterdam, Holland

Dear Sir:

Today I was advised that one F. T. Cheetham of this place has recently filed charges with your Dept. that Mr. Henry C. Balink located in Taos, New Mex. is an undesirable alien, etc.

In this connection I beg to state that I have known Mr. Balink and his wife for the last two years, and for the benefit of your Dept. and in the interest of justice will say that they are both peaceable and industrious Hollanders and have always been pro Ally. Mr. Balink came to Taos to paint Indians. His work is greatly admired and sought after, which has aroused the jealousy of local painters who if not German, their fathers or mothers are!!!!! Balink bought Liberty Bonds to the capacity of his limited means and contributed a valuable drawing after Holbein to the Red Cross of Taos which was placed on exhibition with some twenty paintings donated by local artists. The public were so taken by Mr. Balink's work, that they stated time and time again that it was worth all the others put together. A plan was then made to get rid of him by sending him into the Army with the first draft, though properly he would have been classified with the last.

To defeat this plot Balink took advantage of the President's proclamation and withdrew his application for U.S. citizenship. As regards the standing of the party filing the charges, permit me to suggest that you refer to Hon. Colin Neblett, U.S. Dist. Judge at Santa Fe. This party was discharged as U.S. Commissioner following an investigation of his record here. I should also mention that Balink recently sold a number of his paintings to prominent men of Colorado Springs, which seems to have again aroused the old feelings of antagonism.

In conclusion I will state that I have seen Mr. Balink's discharge papers from the army in Holland, also his passports to this country, also a letter of thanks from the mayor of Amsterdam in the name of the Queen thanking him for his able decorative work which he did for the government. Balink came to this country in Oct. 1914, with a letter of introduction from Count Six of Amsterdam to the Directors of the Metropolitan Museum in New York.

Count Six is known throughout Europe for his philanthropy and for his wonderful art collection and was also a warm personal friend of the late President Roosevelt.

Should you desire information as to myself, it will give me pleasure to refer your Dept. to Senator A. A. Jones and Congressman Hernandez in Washington who are warm personal friends of mine for the last twenty years.

Truly yours,
A. R. Manki

We can come closer to understanding this entire affair by placing it in the context of what was happening in this country in 1919. This was the year of the "Big Red Scare," of lingering war hatred of the "Hun," and of pervasive antiforeigner sentiments.

It is instructive to note that three other prominent foreign-born artists living in Taos, Nicolai Fechin, Leon Gaspard, and Joseph Fleck, were never asked to join the Taos Society of Artists. In defense of the Taos Society of Artists, it should be stated that they felt they were developing an American form of art that necessitated freedom from foreign influences. This belief was affirmed at the annual meeting on July 11, 1919, at which the By-Laws were changed to restrict membership to American citizens.

The role of F. T. Cheetham (mentioned in the above letter) in this controversy remains something of a mystery. He was an attorney in Taos and was at one time vice-president of the Historical Society of New Mexico ("Necrology—Francis T. Cheetham," *New Mexico Historical Review* 21 [April 1946]: 167–68). F. T. Cheetham seems to have been a friend of the Taos Society of Artists. The refreshments at the T.S.A. dance on July 27, 1921 were served by "Mrs. Cheetham," who probably was his wife.

13. Dunton's article, "The Painters of Taos," was very imaginative and well written. It was printed in *The American Magazine of Art* 13 (August 1922): 247–52 and in *El Palacio* 13 (August 15, 1922): 45–46.

14. An article entitled, "Dance by Taos Society" (*El Palacio* 11 [August 1, 1921]: 40) revealed that "the unique invitations, which were all hand drafted, announced further that 'Professor Muller's celebrated orchestra of talented musicians' would furnish the music."

15. Blumenschein was the secretary of a society called "The New Mexico Painters." The Archives of American Art (microfilm roll no. D194) contain several letters written by him as secretary. The stationery of The New Mexico Painters listed the following members in 1924: Frank G. Applegate, Jozef G. Bakos, Gustave Baumann, Ernest L. Blumenschein, William P. Henderson, Victor Higgins, B. J. O. Nordfeldt, Walter Ufer, John Sloan, Andrew Dasburg, Theodore Van Soelen, Randall Davey, and Walter Mruk.

16. In a report on the "Annual Taos Exhibit" in the following year (*El Palacio* 17 [September 1, 1924]: 101–4), the following comment is made:

"The absence of Blumenschein from this year's show has created comment and wonderment."

And two pages later:

"'But where are Blumenschein, Dunton, Groll and Higgins' more than one visitor to the Museum galleries is bound to ask, even though the others have offered so much that is fine, inspiring and praiseworthy."

17. The Taos Society of Artists file at the Museum of New Mexico contains copies of Paul A. F. Walter's correspondence with artists while he was curator of the Fine Arts Museum. Of particular interest is the letter of introduction written by former Chicago mayor Carter H. Harrison, Jr., and carried by E. Martin Hennings on his first trip to New Mexico in 1917:

July 1st 1917.

Secretary New Mexican Historical Society,
Santa Fe, New Mexico,
Dear Sir,

This will be presented to you by Mr. Martin Hennings, one of the most talented of the younger group of Chicago artists, who will spend the summer in your country, looking up suitable motives for his brush. I have suggested to him that he should try to have an exhibition of some of his work in Santa Fe before he returns home. Mr. Hennings' work has been exhibited in many of the recent important national shows. Any assistance you may give him will be appreciated.

Respectfully yours,
Carter H. Harrison

18. One of the letters referred to by J. H. Sharp is in the T.S.A. file. Written to J. H. Sharp by Sam M. Yunt of Kansas City, Missouri, and dated May 5, 1925, the pertinent paragraphs are as follow:

". . . but you have approached a subject which must not only be considered by the Taos Society of Artists but by every other American painter, and that is the prices.

"If you don't mind reading this, I am going into the situation as it comes to me.

"It is a fact that so many of the foreign painters, doing so many fine things, are sending to this country for about one-tenth the price the American artist is asking for his; and it looks as if the American art dealer who does not add to his collection a few of these things is going to be put out of business by the dealers in New York who are carrying these things right along, either ahead of us or behind our exhibitions; but I feel that this is up to the individual artist and I don't take this subject up with any of them individually until I become especially interested in their work and see that it is possible for us to do considerable business with him.

"It is too bad to have the pictures shipped over the country for a whole season and then go back to the studios, and then when someone comes in and offers a price the artist takes it, instead of giving the dealer the price in the beginning and getting his money for his pictures six months before.

"Now, I know this is not the case with you and Mr. Phillips and some of the other boys, but there are a great many fellows in the

East who do this very thing, and it causes the art business to be in very shaky condition."

The prices asked by members of the Taos Society of Artists for their paintings were high, but in relative terms they are probably comparable to the prices asked by top artists today. Correspondence in the Society records indicates that smaller paintings (16" × 20") were priced at about $300 to $350, whereas larger paintings (30" × 36") were priced at $1,200 to $2,000. It should be remembered that during the years that the Society was in existence, a laborer might earn no more than one dollar per day and gold was worth only $20.67 per ounce. By these standards, a $2,000 painting in the 1920s might be comparable to a $30,000 to $50,000 painting in the 1980s.

Index